Reconstruction

Reconstruction

Other books in the At Issue in History series:

Reconstruction

William Dudley, *Book Editor*

Daniel Leone, *President*
Bonnie Szumski, *Publisher*
Scott Barbour, *Managing Editor*

 **AT ISSUE IN HISTORY**

GREENHAVEN
PRESS®

San Diego • Detroit • New York • San Francisco • Cleveland
New Haven, Conn. • Waterville, Maine • London • Munich

THOMSON

★ ™

GALE

LIBRARY OF CONGRESS CATALOGING-IN-PUBLICATION DATA
Reconstruction / William Dudley, book editor.
p. cm. — (At issue in history)
Includes bibliographical references and index.
ISBN 0-7377-1356-9 (lib. : alk. paper) — ISBN 0-7377-1357-7 (pbk. : alk. paper)
1. Reconstruction. I. Dudley, William, 1964– . II. Series.
E668 .R3 2003
975'.041—dc21   2002034720

Contents

Chapter 1: Dealing with the Rebellious South

Chapter 2: Securing the Rights of Blacks

Chapter 3: Evolving Historical Assessments of Reconstruction

Foreword

Historian Robert Weiss defines history simply as "a record and interpretation of past events." Both elements—record and interpretation—are necessary, Weiss argues.

> Names, dates, places, and events are the essence of history. But historical writing is not a compendium of facts. It consists of facts placed in a sequence to tell a connected story. A work of history is not merely a story, however. It also must analyze what happened and *why*—that is, it must interpret the past for the reader.

For example, the events of December 7, 1941, that led President Franklin D. Roosevelt to call it "a date which will live in infamy" are fairly well known and straightforward. A force of Japanese planes and submarines launched a torpedo and bombing attack on American military targets in Pearl Harbor, Hawaii. The surprise assault sank five battleships, disabled or sank fourteen additional ships, and left almost twenty-four hundred American soldiers and sailors dead. On the following day, the United States formally entered World War II when Congress declared war on Japan.

These facts and consequences were almost immediately communicated to the American people who heard reports about Pearl Harbor and President Roosevelt's response on the radio. All realized that this was an important and pivotal event in American and world history. Yet the news from Pearl Harbor raised many unanswered questions. Why did Japan decide to launch such an offensive? Why were the attackers so successful in catching America by surprise? What did the attack reveal about the two nations, their people, and their leadership? What were its causes, and what were its effects? Political leaders, academic historians, and students look to learn the basic facts of historical events and to read the intepretations of these events by many different sources, both primary and secondary, in order to develop a more complete picture of the event in a historical context.

In the case of Pearl Harbor, several important questions surrounding the event remain in dispute, most notably the role of President Roosevelt. Some historians have blamed his policies for deliberately provoking Japan to attack in order to propel America into World War II; a few have gone so far as to accuse him of knowing of the impending attack but not informing others. Other historians, examining the same event, have exonerated the president of such charges, arguing that the historical evidence does not support such a theory.

The Greenhaven At Issue in History series recognizes that many important historical events have been interpreted differently and in some cases remain shrouded in controversy. Each volume features a collection of articles that focus on a topic that has sparked controversy among eyewitnesses, contemporary observers, and historians. An introductory essay sets the stage for each topic by presenting background and context. Several chapters then examine different facets of the subject at hand with readings chosen for their diversity of opinion. Each selection is preceded by a summary of the author's main points and conclusions. A bibliography is included for those students interested in pursuing further research. An annotated table of contents and thorough index help readers to quickly locate material of interest. Taken together, the contents of each of the volumes in the Greenhaven At Issue in History series will help students become more discriminating and thoughtful readers of history.

Introduction

Reconstruction refers both to the historical period immediately following America's Civil War and the political process by which the states of the defeated Confederacy were restored to the Union. Reconstruction has long been one of the most controversial eras of American history. The challenges—and opportunities—facing the nation after the Civil War were immense. In addition to the problems inherent in rebuilding the American South from the ravages of war, America had to confront two significant and fundamental questions. One was how best to reintegrate the defeated Southern states into America's federal system of government. The second was how best to integrate 4 million blacks into an American society in which they were no longer slaves. These two questions were at the heart of most controversies during Reconstruction and remain at the center of differing assessments of the period by historians.

Wartime Reconstruction (1863–1865)

Debates over the central questions of Reconstruction began even before the war ended. One matter of continuing dispute was the legal status of the states—Alabama, Arkansas, Florida, Georgia, Louisiana, Mississippi, North Carolina, South Carolina, Tennessee, Texas, and Virginia—that had declared their intention to secede (withdraw) from the United States. Some Northerners believed that these states should be treated as federal territories in which questions of governance would be ultimately decided by Congress. Others held that because secession was illegal, the states had never really withdrawn from the Union. They held that following the Union victory (and the punishment of individual traitors), the states should be quickly restored and given the same leeway that America's national government had always given state governments to conduct their internal affairs.

The second central question involved the fate of America's 4 million slaves. Their emancipation was not a goal of the North at the beginning of the Civil War. In July 1861

Congress passed the Crittenden Resolutions, asserting that its war aim was reunion, not reconstruction of race relations. However, as the war persisted and its costs grew beyond everyone's expectations, so did its goals. Abolitionists found their cause joined by those who believed that freeing the slaves would help weaken the Confederacy and win the war—and would give the costly conflict a worthy sense of purpose.

The leaders of the antislavery cause in Congress were members of the Republican Party and came to be known as Radical Republicans. Their leaders, who included Charles Sumner in the Senate and Thaddeus Stevens in the House, believed that abolition was not enough and that the freed slaves should have full rights of U.S. citizenship, including the right to vote. Radical Republicans argued that, once the war ended, Southern governments should be "reconstructed" to provide such rights for all people before restoration to the Union.

In January 1863 Lincoln cheered the Radical Republicans with his Emancipation Proclamation, which made ending slavery a Civil War goal. In December 1863, however, many of the same people were disappointed when the president announced his plans for Reconstruction. Lincoln, who dismissed the question of whether the states had actually withdrawn from the Union as a "pernicious abstraction," offered a presidential pardon to Southerners (except ranking Confederate leaders) who took an oath swearing loyalty to the Union and supporting slavery emancipation. Under his plan, a new state government and constitution could be formed when 10 percent of the state's voters had been thus politically rehabilitated. Under Lincoln's "Ten Percent Plan," state governments were created in Union-occupied Arkansas, Louisiana, and Tennessee.

Lincoln's plan drew criticism from Radical Republicans in Congress, who believed that it was too mild and did not do enough to punish the South or protect the status of blacks. In 1864 they passed their own version of Reconstruction—sponsored by Benjamin Wade and Henry Winter Davis and known as the Wade-Davis Bill—that required a majority of a state's population to affirm loyalty to the Union before a civilian state government could be organized. The plan would have barred all those who had taken arms against the Union from voting and would have compelled the new states to abolish slavery. Lincoln refused to sign the measure. By the end of the Civil War, the questions arising from the Wade-Davis Bill and its veto remained unsettled. Whether Lincoln and Congress could have settled their differences is an unsolvable question. On April 14, one week after the Civil War ended, the president was assassinated.

Presidential Reconstruction (1865–1867)

Lincoln's death left America's Reconstruction policy in the hands of his vice president, Andrew Johnson. Johnson, a Tennessee politician, was the only senator from a seceding state to stay personally loyal to the Union. A member of the Democratic Party, he had been placed on the ticket in 1864 as a balancing measure. His views on states' rights and the need to limit political power to whites placed him in opposition to Radical Republicans in Congress.

In May 1865, while Congress was not in session, Johnson put his plans on Reconstruction in effect by issuing a series of presidential proclamations. He offered presidential pardons to all but a few former Confederates, appointed provisional governors, and outlined conditions for Southern state readmission. These conditions included ending slavery, repudiating any right of states to secede, and nullifying Confederate war debts. Blacks were not given a role in the process of creating the reconstituted state governments.

During the summer and fall of 1865, new state governments were organized throughout the South. However, the actions of these new governments alarmed many in the North, especially Republicans in Congress. Many states elected prominent former Confederate leaders to government posts. They also enacted a series of laws, known as "Black Codes," aimed at controlling the ex-slave population. These laws forced blacks to sign year-long labor contracts, authorized the whipping of black workers, and allowed states to jail unemployed blacks as vagrants and hire them out to private employers. Other laws forbade blacks from owning or leasing their own farms and seeking jobs other than as farmhands or domestic servants.

Opposition in Congress

When Congress finally convened in December 1865, it refused admission to the senators and representatives from the states that were "restored" under Johnson's program.

Determined to chart their own Reconstruction program, members established the Joint Committee on Reconstruction to investigate conditions in the South and to advise Congress in setting Reconstruction policies. These actions set off a power struggle between Congress and Johnson, who contended that Congress had no right to set policy until Southern congressmen and senators were admitted.

The Black Codes passed by the Southern states were one reason why Congress refused to seat the newly elected Southern members. Political considerations also played a part. The secession of the Southern states and withdrawal of their representatives in 1861 had left the Republican Party in firm control of Congress during the Civil War. Republicans feared that with the readmission of the Southern states to Congress, the Democratic Party would take over. The South would also get increased representation in Congress, based on the full accounting of their black population, even though most blacks were still denied the right to vote.

In 1866 Congress (minus the barred Southern representatives) passed two major laws over President Johnson's veto—the first major laws to be so approved in American history. One measure extended the life of the Freedmen's Bureau, an agency Congress created in 1865 to oversee the former slaves' transition to freedom. The 1866 Civil Rights Act defined all persons born in the United States as citizens, thus granting the ex-slaves U.S. citizenship.

To further secure the legal status and civil rights of blacks, Congress passed the Fourteenth Amendment to the Constitution. The amendment contained several elements of the Radical Republicans' agenda. The first section set up a national definition of citizenship and declared all persons born or naturalized in the United States to be citizens. The second section provided that if a state denied suffrage to its adult male inhabitants, its representation in the House of Representatives and the electoral college would be proportionately cut. A third section barred all former federal and state officials who had "engaged in insurrection" from holding public office.

The Radical Republican Program for Reconstruction (1867–1877)

Congress demanded that the Southern states ratify the Fourteenth Amendment before they could be readmitted.

When all of the Southern states except Tennessee refused to ratify the Fourteenth Amendment, the Radical Republicans in Congress (whose numbers had been bolstered by the 1866 elections) essentially started over. With enough votes to easily override President Johnson's continued vetoes, Congress passed the Reconstruction Acts of 1867. The laws dissolved the state governments formed under Johnson's plan and divided the South into five military districts under federal military rule. Under these auspices new state governments were constructed, with blacks eligible to vote, but many (white) former Confederates barred from participating. By 1870 all of the former Confederate states had been readmitted to the Union, and most were under the control of the Republican Party. In addition, by 1870 both the Fourteenth Amendment and the Fifteenth Amendment, which outlawed race barriers to voting, had been added to the Constitution. A Republican president—former general Ulysses S. Grant— was in office (Johnson had been impeached by Congress in 1868; although he was not removed from office, his efforts to obstruct the Radical Republicans were finished).

The people who ran the Republican governments of the former Confederate states generally belonged to one of three groups: blacks, "carpetbaggers," and "scalawags." Blacks constituted the largest groups of voters, but South Carolina was the only state with a black majority in its legislature. *Carpetbagger* was the term given to former North-

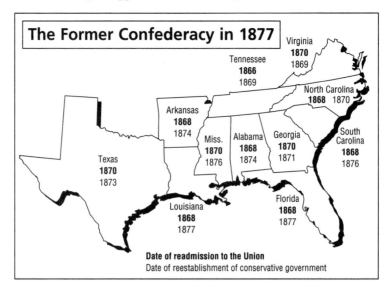

The Former Confederacy in 1877

Virginia
1870
1869

Tennessee
1866
1869

North Carolina
1868 1870

Arkansas
1868
1874

Miss.
1870
1876

Alabama
1868
1874

Georgia
1870
1871

South Carolina
1868
1876

Texas
1870
1873

Louisiana
1868
1877

Florida
1868
1877

Date of readmission to the Union
Date of reestablishment of conservative government

ern residents (many of them Civil War veterans) who moved south to pursue economic and political opportunities. *Scalawags* was a derisive term given to Southern whites who participated in the governments; many came from poor backgrounds and resented the plantation owners who had politically dominated the antebellum South.

These state governments did achieve a number of goals. They expanded social services, established public school systems (previously lacking in the South), and attempted to promote economic development. However, many whites never fully accepted their legitimacy and blamed government corruption and incompetence for the continued economic hardships the region experienced after the Civil War. Many also resented the fact that former slaves now governed them. The state governments remained dependent on federal military support and the enforcement of federal laws in order to function.

White Resistance and the End of Reconstruction

By 1871 whites in many parts of the South had stepped up their resistance to the new state authorities. Secret organizations, the best known of which was the Ku Klux Klan, engaged in acts of terror against blacks, carpetbaggers, and scalawags. Local authorities were afraid to call out local militia troops (many of whom were black) for fear of starting race riots. Congress responded to the crisis by passing several laws making such terror tactics federal crimes and sending in more federal troops to enforce them. However, many Northerners were becoming increasingly tired of Reconstruction and disillusioned with the continued reports of disorder in the South. The national Republican Party became more conservative as former Radicals died or retired. In 1874 Democrats won control of the House of Representatives for the first time since the Civil War—another indication that national support for Reconstruction goals was waning.

As national support for Reconstruction declined, Republican state governments fell one by one as white voters elected Democratic governors and representatives in elections often marred by fraud and violence. By 1876 just three Southern states—Florida, Louisiana, and South Carolina—had Republican governments. The 1876 presidential election between Republican Rutherford B. Hayes and Democrat Samuel J. Tilden was extremely close; its outcome hinged on the disputed election results of the three remaining Southern states with Reconstruction governments. Hayes was declared the victor; in 1877 he announced that remaining federal troops would be withdrawn from the South. The remaining Republican governments soon came under Democratic control, making the Democratic Party's "Solid South" hold on the region one of the legacies of Reconstruction.

By 1877 the question of how to restore the Confederate states to the Union had been settled. The states had all rejoined the Union and had taken their place again as part of the United States of America. As memories of the Civil War faded, national concerns turned to new issues, such as industrial development and western expansion.

Reconstruction's results in creating an African American citizenry are mixed. The gains blacks experienced during Reconstruction in voting and civil rights soon vanished as state governments, free of federal interference, passed laws to segregate public schools and facilities and limit black voting rights. The South continued to violate the civil rights of blacks for decades after 1877. However, Reconstruction's legacy also includes the Fourteenth and Fifteenth Amendments to the Constitution, which became the legal basis for the Civil Rights movement during the 1950s and 1960s.

Chapter 1

Dealing with the Rebellious South

1

The South Can Be Safely Restored to the Union

Benjamin C. Truman

During the Civil War, Benjamin C. Truman worked as a newspaper reporter and staff aide to Andrew Johnson when Johnson was military governor of Tennessee. In 1865 Johnson, then president, asked Truman to visit the South and submit a report on conditions there. In contrast to the views of Carl Schurz, who was sent on a similar assignment, Truman concludes that most Southerners had accepted the outcome of the Civil War and were ready to manage their own affairs without interference from Union soldiers. He also defends the attitudes and actions of former slave owners toward the newly freed slaves.

I record it as my profound conviction, gathered from hundreds of intimate and friendly conversations with leading men in the south, that there are not fifty respectable politicians who still believe in the "constitutional right of secession," though they are exceedingly slow to acknowledge it in public speeches or published articles. Our conversations generally ended with the confession—which to me was entirely satisfactory, as meaning much more than was intended—"Whatever may be said about the *right* of secession, the thing itself may as well be laid aside, for it is certainly *not practicable*, and probably *never will be*." I believe there is the most charity, and by far the most correctness, in that reasoning which accounts in this way for the extreme reluctance that has been exhibited in most of the conventions against declaring the act of secession null and void

Benjamin C. Truman, *Senate Executive Documents*, #43, 39th Congress, I Session, 1865–1866.

from the beginning. They will willingly concede that the *right* of secession *does not now* exist, provided only they are allowed to assert that *it did at that time*, which is simply a petty device of sorely humbled and defeated men to save their wounded pride. . . .

There are not fifty respectable politicians who still believe in the "constitutional right of secession."

There is a prevalent disposition not to associate too freely with northern men, or to receive them into the circles of society; but it is far from insurmountable. Over southern society, as over every other, woman reigns supreme, and they are more imbittered against those whom they deem the authors of all their calamities than are their brothers, sons and husbands. It is a noteworthy ethnological fact, and one I have often observed, that of the younger generation the southern women are much superior to the southern men both in intellect and energy; and their ascendency over society is correspondingly great. . . .

But the stories and rumors to the effect that northern men are bitterly persecuted and compelled to abandon the country, I pronounce false. If northern men go south they must expect for a while to be treated with neglect, and sometimes with contempt; but if they refrain from bitter political discussions, and conduct themselves with ordinary discretion, they soon overcome these prejudices and are treated with respect. The accounts that are from time to time flooded over the country in regard to southern cruelty and intolerance toward northerners are mostly false. I could select many districts, however, particularly in northern Texas and portions of Mississippi, where northern men could not at present live with any degree of self-respect. There are also localities in many of the southern States where it would be dangerous for a northern man to live, but they are exceptional, and are about equally unsafe for any man who possesses attractive property. For some unknown cause a large number of persons are engaged in writing and circulating falsehoods. For some unpatriotic purpose or other, reports of an incendiary character concerning the southern people are transmitted north. To learn the falseness of these reports one needs only to obtain the facts. I am personally acquainted with most of the officers of a hundred-odd regiments of volunteers, and out of these I could name thirty regiments one-half of whose officers and many of the men have returned to the south, and as many more that have left large numbers there upon being disbanded. Hundreds, even, of the officers of colored regiments—the most offensive to the south—have remained there and entered into business, the most of them having rented plantations and employing their old soldiers. Large numbers of ex-federal and ex-confederate officers are engaged together in mercantile pursuits and in cotton-planting. Nearly all of the cotton plantations in Florida are being run by such parties. The banks of the Mississippi are lined with plantations which have been leased by northern men and federal officers. . . . Fourteen officers of a colored (Kentucky) regiment are engaged in planting and raising cotton near Victoria, Texas. . . . In all of these connexions the utmost harmony prevails. Notwithstanding the above facts—and I could multiply them—I maintain that in many sections of the south there is a wide-spread hostility to northern men, which, however, in nine cases out of ten, is speedily dispelled by individual contact, and the exercise of a generous regard for private opinions. In fine, I will say that all who can be spared from the industry of the north to go south can readily find places of business where they can live in quiet and prosperity. . . .

Loyalty of the States

Though there is no district in Florida that can strictly be called loyal in contradistinction to all others, yet I found the feeling of the people in that State much better and more encouraging than in Georgia, which is overrun with politicians, many of whom seem to defy the government and its authority. Alabama is in a much better condition than Georgia, and its state of affairs is extremely encouraging. Mississippi, from one end to the other, of all the States which I visited, is far behindhand in her tokens of loyalty; there is an unmistakable flow of ill feeling in that State, although I witnessed no exhibitions of unmitigated disloyalty; on the whole, the people of that State fear the authority of the United States more than they respect it. In Louisiana there is an encouraging element of loyalty which is experiencing a healthy increase. Tennessee evidenced in a great degree the most flourishing signs of loyalty; I do not think there are ten men in that State at present who could be induced to favor a dissolution of the Union, not even indeed, if such a thing should be peaceably permitted. There is a healthy intercourse between all classes in Arkansas, and it seemed to me to occupy nearly the identical position of Tennessee.

Relations with Former Slaves

I will now proceed to the second great topic, to wit: "The freedmen and their affairs."

Almost the only key that furnishes a satisfactory solution to the southern question in its relations to the negro, that gives a reasonable explanation to the treatment which he receives and the estimation in which he is held, is found in the fact—too often forgotten in considering this matter—that the people from their earliest days have regarded slavery as his proper estate, and emancipation as a bane to his happiness. That a vast majority of the southern people honestly entertain this opinion no one who travels among them for eight months can doubt. . . .

Resulting as a proper corollary from these premises, we have seen various laws passed in some of the States, but more particularly in Mississippi—which State, I am bound to say, has displayed the most illiberal spirit toward the freedmen of all the south—imposing heavy taxes on negroes engaged in the various trades, amounting to a virtual prohibition. Petty, unjust, and discriminating licenses are levied in this State upon mechanics, storekeepers, and various artisans. Following the same absurd train of argument that one will hear in the north in regard to the "proper sphere of women," their legislature and their common councils contend that in these pursuits the negro is out of his place; that he is not adapted to such labors, but only the ruder tasks of the field. What are known as the "poor whites" sustain, in fact originate, this legislation, upon the insane dread they share in common with certain skilled laborers at the north, of competition and an overcrowding of the supply. This folly and injustice on the part of the lawmakers is being corrected in many sections. The negro, however, has not been discouraged, even in Mississippi; his industry and his thrift are overleaping all obstacles, and in Jackson there are at least two colored craftsmen of most kinds to one of the whites. . . .

I believe that in some of the most interior districts, especially in Texas, the substance of slavery still remains, in the form of the bondage of custom, of fear, and of inferiority; but nowhere are there any negroes so ignorant of the great change that has taken place as to submit to the lash. In no place did I hear the slightest allusion to any punishment of this sort having been inflicted since the rebellion ended. In every case it was violent stabbing or shooting, resulting from a personal encounter. The negro was aware of his rights, and was defending them. His friends need never fear his re-enslavement; it never can, never will take place. His head is filled with the idea of freedom, and anything but the most insidious and blandishing encroachments upon his freedom he will perceive and resist. The planters everywhere complain of his "demoralization" in this respect.

The accounts that are from time to time flooded over the country in regard to southern . . . intolerance toward northerners are mostly false.

As to the personal treatment received by the negro at the hands of the southern people there is wide-spread misapprehension. It is not his former master, as a general thing, that is his worst enemy, but quite the contrary. I have talked earnestly with hundreds of old slave-owners, and seen them move among their former "chattels," and I am not mistaken. The feeling with which a very large majority of them regard the negro is one of genuine commiseration, although it is not a sentiment much elevated above that with which they would look upon a suffering animal for which they had formed an attachment. Last summer the negroes, exulting in their new-found freedom, as was to have been expected, were gay, thoughtless, and improvident; and, as a consequence, when the winter came hundreds of them felt the pinchings of want, and many perished. The old planters have often pointed out to me numerous instances of calamity that had come under their own observation in the case of their former slaves and others. . . .

It is the former slave-owners who are the best friends the negro has in the south—those who, heretofore, have provided for his mere physical comfort, generally with sufficient means, though entirely neglecting his better nature, while it is the "poor whites" that are his enemies. It is from these he suffers most. In a state of slavery they hated him; and, now that he is free, there is no striking abatement of this sentiment, and the former master no longer feels called by the instincts of interest to extend that protection that he once did. On the streets, by the roadside, in his wretched hut, in the field of labor—everywhere, the inoffensive negro is exposed to their petty and contemptible persecutions; while, on the other hand, I have known instances where the respectable, substantial people of a community have united together to keep guard over a house in which the negroes were taking their amusement, and from which, a few nights before, they had been rudely driven by white vagabonds, who found pleasure in their fright and suffering. I reiterate, that the former owners, as a class, are the negroes' best friends in the south, although many of this class diligently strive to discourage the freedmen from any earnest efforts to promote their higher welfare. When one believes that a certain race of beings are incapable of advancement, he is very prone to withhold the means of that advancement. And it is in this form that a species of slavery will longest be per-petuated—it is in these strongholds that it will last die out. I am pretty sure that there is not a single negro in the whole south who is not receiving pay for his labor according to his own contract; but, as a general thing, the freedmen are en-couraged to collect about the old mansion in their little quarters, labor for their former master for set terms, receiv-ing, besides their pay, food, quarters, and medical atten-dance, and thus continuing on in their former state of de-pendence. The cruelties of slavery, and all of its outward forms, have entirely passed away; but, as might have been expected, glimmerings of its vassalage, its subserviency, and its helplessness, linger.

It is the result of my observation, also, not only that the planters, generally, are far better friends to the negro than the poor whites, but also better than a majority of northern men who go south to rent plantations—at least, they show more patience in dealing with him. The northerner is prac-tical, energetic, economical, and thrifty—the negro is slow, awkward, wasteful, and slovenly; he causes his new em-ployer to lose his patience, to seize hold and attempt to per-form, himself, what he sees so badly executed. The south-erner is accustomed to the ways of slaves from his youth up; hence he is languidly and good-naturedly indifferent; or, at most, vents his displeasure in empty fuming. The northern employer is accustomed to see laborers who are vigorous and industrious; he knows the extent of a full day's labor, and he expects all to perform the amount; the southern man has always been compelled to employ two or three to do the work of one, and is more indulgent. It is the almost universal testimony of the negroes themselves, who have been under the supervision of both classes—and I have talked with many with a view to this point—that they prefer to labor for a southern employer. This is not by any means to be construed to mean that they desire to return to slavery—not by any consideration, for the thought of freedom is dearer to their hearts than to any other people.

2

The South Needs Social Reconstruction Before It Can Rejoin the Union

Carl Schurz

In 1865 President Andrew Johnson sent a delegation to investigate conditions in the former Confederate states and to report back to him. One of the commissioners was Carl Schurz, a German immigrant who had risen to the rank of major general during the Civil War. Schurz's report, excerpted here, concludes that the attitude of most Southerners is anything but conciliatory. Southern leaders, he reports, continue to mistreat the newly freed black slaves and are reluctant to comply with Reconstruction measures. He questions whether Johnson's lenient policies toward the former Confederate states will work. Schurz fell out of favor with Johnson due to this report, but his conclusions were shared and publicized by Radical Republicans in Congress.

I n seeking remedies . . . we ought to keep in view, above all, the nature of the problem which is to be solved. As to what is commonly termed "reconstruction," it is not only the political machinery of the States and their constitutional relations to the General Government, but the whole organism of Southern society that must be reconstructed, or rather constructed anew, so as to bring it in harmony with the rest of American society. The difficulties of this task are not to be considered overcome when the people of the South take the oath of allegiance and elect governors and

Carl Schurz, *Condition of the South*, Washington, DC, 1866.

legislatures and members of Congress and militia captains. That this would be done had become certain as soon as the surrenders of the Southern armies had made further resistance impossible, and nothing in the world was left, even to the most uncompromising rebel, but to submit or to emigrate. It was also natural that they should avail themselves of every chance offered them to resume control of their home affairs and to regain their influence in the Union. But this can hardly be called the first step towards the solution of the true problem, and it is a fair question to ask, whether the hasty gratification of their desire to resume such control would not create new embarrassments.

> *It is not only the political machinery of the States and their constitutional relations to the General Government, but the whole organism of Southern society that must be reconstructed.*

The true nature of the difficulties of the situation is this: The General Government of the republic has, by proclaiming the emancipation of the slaves, commenced a great social revolution in the South, but has, as yet, not completed it. Only the negative part of it is accomplished. The slaves are emancipated in point of form, but free labor has not yet been put in the place of slavery in point of fact. And now, in the midst of this critical period of transition, the power which originated the revolution is expected to turn over its whole future development to another power which from the beginning was hostile to it and has never yet entered into its spirit, leaving the class in whose favor it was made completely without power to protect itself and to take an influential part in that development. The history of the world will be searched in vain for a proceeding similar to this which did not lead either to a rapid and violent reaction, or to the most serious trouble and civil disorder. It cannot be said that the conduct of the Southern people since the close of the war has exhibited such extraordinary wisdom and self-abnegation as to make them an exception to the rule.

Changing from Slavery to Free Labor

In my despatches from the South I repeatedly expressed the opinion that the people were not yet in a frame of mind to legislate calmly and understandingly upon the subject of free negro labor. And this I reported to be the opinion of some of our most prominent military commanders and other observing men. It is, indeed, difficult to imagine circumstances more unfavorable for the development of a calm and unprejudiced public opinion than those under which the Southern people are at present laboring. The war has not only defeated their political aspirations, but it has broken up their whole social organization. When the rebellion was put down, they found themselves not only conquered in a political and military sense, but economically ruined. The planters, who represented the wealth of the Southern country, are partly laboring under the severest embarrassments, partly reduced to absolute poverty. Many who are stripped of all available means, and have nothing but their land, cross their arms in gloomy despondency, incapable of rising in a manly resolution. Others, who still possess means, are at a loss how to use them, as their old way of doing things is, by the abolition of slavery, rendered impracticable, at least where the military arm of the government has enforced emancipation. Others are still trying to go on in the old way, and that old way is in fact the only one they understand, and in which they have any confidence. Only a minority is trying to adopt the new order of things. A large number of the plantations, probably a considerable majority of the more valuable estates, is under heavy mortgages, and the owners know that, unless they retrieve their fortunes in a comparatively short space of time, their property will pass out of their hands. Almost all are, to some extent, embarrassed. The nervous anxiety which such a state of things produces extends also to those classes of society which, although not composed of planters, were always in close business connection with the planting interest, and there was hardly a branch of commerce or industry in the South which was not directly or indirectly so connected. Besides, the Southern soldiers, when returning from the war, did not, like the Northern soldiers, find a prosperous community which merely waited for their arrival to give them remunerative employment. They found, many of them, their homesteads destroyed, their farms devastated, their families in distress; and those that were less unfortunate found, at all events, an impoverished and exhausted community which had but little to offer them. Thus a great many have been thrown upon the world to shift as best they can. They must do something honest or dishonest, and must do it soon, to make a living, and their prospects are, at present, not very bright. Thus that nervous anxiety to hastily repair broken fortunes, and to prevent still greater ruin and distress, embraces nearly all classes, and imprints upon all the movements of the social body a morbid character.

In which direction will these people be most apt to turn their eyes? Leaving the prejudice of race out of the question, from early youth they have been acquainted with but one system of labor, and with that one system they have been in the habit of identifying all their interests. They know of no way to help themselves but the one they are accustomed to. Another system of labor is presented to them, which, however, owing to circumstances which they do not appreciate, appears at first in an improvising light. To try it they consider an experiment which they cannot afford to make while their wants are urgent. They have not reasoned calmly enough to convince themselves that the trial must be made. It is, indeed, not wonderful that, under such circumstances, they should study, not how to introduce and develop free labor, but how to avoid its introduction, and how to return as much and as quickly as possible to something like the older order of things. Nor is it wonderful that such studies should find an expression in their attempts at legislation. But the circumstance that this tendency is natural does not render it less dangerous and objectionable. The practical question presents itself: Is the immediate restoration of the late rebel States to absolute self-control so necessary that it must be done even at the risk of endangering one of the great results of the war, and of bringing on in those States insurrection or anarchy, or would it not be better to postpone that restoration until such dangers are passed? If, as long as the change from slavery to free labor is known to the Southern people only by its destructive results, these people must be expected to throw obstacles in its way, would it not seem necessary that the movement of social "reconstruction" be kept in the right channel by the hand of the power which originated the change, until that change can have disclosed some of its beneficial effects?

False Hopes

It is certain that every success of free negro labor will augment the number of its friends, and disarm some of the prejudices and assumptions of its opponents. I am convinced one good harvest made by unadulterated free labor in the South would have a far better effect than all the oaths that have been taken, and all the ordinances that have as yet been passed by Southern conventions. But how can such a result be attained? The facts enumerated in this report, as well as the news we receive from the South from day to day, must make it evident to every unbiased observer that unadulterated free labor cannot be had at present, unless the National Government holds its protective and controlling hand over it. It appears, also, that the more efficient this protection of free labor against all disturbing and reactionary influences, the sooner may such a satisfactory result be looked for. One reason why the Southern people are so slow in accommodating themselves to the new order of things is, that they confidently expect soon to be permitted to regulate matters according to their own notions. Every concession made to them by the Government has been taken as an encouragement to persevere in this hope, and, unfortunately for them, this hope is nourished by influences from other parts of the country. Hence their anxiety to have their State governments restored *at once*, to have the troops withdrawn, and the Freedmen's Bureau abolished, although a good many discerning men know well that, in view of the lawless spirit still prevailing, it would be far better for them to have the general order of society firmly maintained by the Federal power until things have arrived at a final settlement. Had, from the beginning, the conviction been forced upon them that the adulteration of the new order of things by the admixture of elements belonging to the system of slavery would under no circumstances be permitted, a much larger number would have launched their energies into the new channel, and, seeing that they could do no "better," faithfully coöperated with the Government. It is hope which fixes them in their perverse notions. That hope nourished or fully gratified, they will persevere in the same direction. That hope destroyed, a great many will, by the force of necessity, at once accommodate themselves to the logic of the change. If, therefore, the National Government firmly and unequivocally announces its policy not to give up the control of the free-labor reform until it is finally accomplished, the progress of that reform will undoubtedly be far more rapid and far less difficult than it will be if the attitude of the

Government is such as to permit contrary hopes to be indulged in. . . .

Negro Suffrage

In discussing the matter of negro suffrage I deemed it my duty to confine myself strictly to the practical aspects of the subject. I have, therefore, not touched its moral merits nor discussed the question whether the National Government is competent to enlarge the elective franchise in the States lately in rebellion by its own act; I deem it proper, however, to offer a few remarks on the assertion frequently put forth, that the franchise is likely to be extended to the colored man by the voluntary action of the Southern whites themselves. My observation leads me to a contrary opinion. Aside from a very few enlightened men, I found but one class of people in favor of the enfranchisement of the blacks: it was the class of Unionists who found themselves politically ostracised and looked upon the enfranchisement of the loyal negroes as the salvation of the whole loyal element. But their numbers and influence are sadly insufficient to secure such a result. The masses are strongly opposed to colored suffrage; anybody that dares to advocate it is stigmatized as a dangerous fanatic; nor do I deem it probable that in the ordinary course of things prejudices will wear off to such an extent as to make it a popular measure. Outside of Louisiana only one gentleman who occupied a prominent political position in the South expressed to me an opinion favorable to it. He declared himself ready to vote for an amendment to the constitution of his State bestowing the right of suffrage upon all male citizens without distinction of color who could furnish evidence of their ability to read and write, without, however, disfranchising those who are now voters and are not able to fulfill that condition. This gentleman is now a member of one of the State conventions, but I presume he will not risk his political standing in the South by moving such an amendment in that body.

The only manner in which, in my opinion, the Southern people can be induced to grant to the freedman some measure of self-protecting power in the form of suffrage, is to make it a condition precedent to "readmission."

I have to notice one pretended remedy for the disorders now agitating the South, which seems to have become the favorite plan of some prominent public men. It is that the whole colored population of the South should be transported to some place where they could live completely separated from the whites. It is hardly necessary to discuss, not only the question of right and justice, but the difficulties and expense necessarily attending the deportation of nearly four millions of people. But it may be asked, what would become of the industry of the South for many years, if the bulk of its laboring population were taken away? The South stands in need of an increase and not of a diminution of its laboring force to repair the losses and disasters of the last four years. Much is said of imported European laborers and Northern men; this is the favorite idea of many planters who want such immigrants to work on their plantations. . . .

The slaves are emancipated in point of form, but free labor has not yet been put in the place of slavery in point of fact.

But whatever the efficiency of such expedients may be, the true problem remains, not how to remove the colored man from his present field of labor, but how to make him, where he is, a true freeman and an intelligent and useful citizen. The means are simple: protection by the Government until his political and social status enables him to protect himself, offering to his legitimate ambition the stimulant of a perfectly fair chance in life, and granting to him the rights which in every just organization of society are coupled with corresponding duties.

The South Falls Short

I may sum up all I have said in a few words. If nothing were necessary but to restore the machinery of government in the States lately in rebellion in point of form, the movements made to that end by the people of the South might be considered satisfactory. But if it is required that the Southern people should also accommodate themselves to the results of the war in point of spirit, those movements fall far short of what must be insisted upon.

The loyalty of the masses and most of the leaders of the Southern people, consists in submission to necessity. There is, except in individual instances, an entire absence of that national spirit which forms the basis of true loyalty and patriotism.

The emancipation of the slaves is submitted to only in so far as chattel slavery in the old form could not be kept up. But although the freedman is no longer considered the property of the individual master, he is considered the slave of society, and all independent State legislation will share the tendency to make him such. The ordinances abolishing slavery passed by the conventions under the pressure of circumstances, will not be looked upon as barring the establishment of a new form of servitude.

One reason why the Southern people are so slow in accommodating themselves to the new order of things is, that they confidently expect soon to be permitted to regulate matters according to their own notions.

Practical attempts on the part of the Southern people to deprive the negro of his rights as a freeman may result in bloody collisions, and will certainly plunge Southern society into restless fluctuations and anarchical confusion. Such evils can be prevented only by continuing the control of the National Government in the States lately in rebellion until free labor is fully developed and firmly established, and the advantages and blessings of the new order of things have disclosed themselves. This desirable result will be hastened by a firm declaration on the part of the Government, that national control in the South will not cease until such results are secured. Only in this way can that security be established in the South which will render numerous immigration possible, and such immigration would materially aid a favorable development of things.

The solution of the problem would be very much facilitated by enabling all the loyal and free-labor elements in the South to exercise a healthy influence upon legislation. It will hardly be possible to secure the freedman against oppressive class legislation and private persecution, unless he be endowed with a certain measure of political power.

As to the future peace and harmony of the Union, it is of the highest importance that the people lately in rebellion be not permitted to build up another "peculiar institution" whose spirit is in conflict with the fundamental principles of our political system; for as long as they cherish interests peculiar to them in preference to those they have in common with the rest of the American people, their loyalty to the Union will always be uncertain.

I desire not to be understood as saying that there are no well-meaning men among those who were compromised in the rebellion. There are many, but neither their number nor their influence is strong enough to control the manifest tendency of the popular spirit.

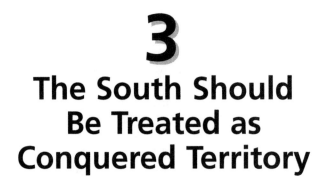

3

The South Should Be Treated as Conquered Territory

Thaddeus Stevens

A central issue after the Civil War ended was what the terms should be for restoring the Southern states to the Union. The controversy over that question also reflected a power struggle between President Andrew Johnson, a former Democrat, and Radical Republicans in Congress over who should determine the course of Reconstruction. A leading spokesperson for the Radical Republicans was Thaddeus Stevens, a Pennsylvanian who served in the House of Representatives.

On December 18, 1865, Stevens addressed Congress, outlining some of his views on how the states should be restored. During the previous months, when Congress was not in session, Johnson had issued a series of presidential proclamations establishing steps under which the Southern states were to be restored to the Union. These steps included the abolition of slavery and the repudiation of secession and Confederate debts, but did not include civil rights or suffrage reforms for blacks. This program was unsatisfactory to Stevens, who believed that the former Confederate states should be treated as conquered territory rather than as full and equal states. In his speech, Stevens argues that Congress, not the president, possesses the authority to determine how and when the former Confederate states will be able to rejoin the Union. He expresses concern that former Rebels are being permitted back into power, while newly freed slaves are being excluded.

Thaddeus Stevens, speech delivered before Congress, December 18, 1865.

A candid examination of the power and proper principles of reconstruction can be offensive to no one, and may possibly be profitable by exciting inquiry. One of the suggestions of the message which we are now considering [President Johnson's December 18, 1865, message to Congress] has special references to this. Perhaps it is the principle most interesting to the people at this time. The President assumes, what no one doubts, that the late rebel States have lost their constitutional relations with the Union, and are incapable of representation in Congress, except by permission of the Government. It matters but little, with this admission, whether you call them States out of the Union, and now conquered territories, or assert that because the Constitution forbids them to do what they did do, that they are therefore only dead as to all national and political action, and will remain so until the government shall breathe into them the breath of life anew and permit them to occupy their former position. In other words, that they are not out of the Union, but are only dead carcasses lying within the Union. In either case, it is very plain that it requires the action of Congress to enable them to form a State government and send representatives to Congress. Nobody, I believe, pretends that with their old constitutions and frames of government they can be permitted to claim their old rights under the Constitution. They have torn their constitutional States into atoms, and built on their foundations fabrics of a totally different character. Dead men cannot raise themselves. Dead States cannot restore their own existence "as it was." Whose especial duty is it to do it? In whom does the Constitution place the power? Not in the judicial branch of the Government, for it only adjudicates and does not prescribe laws. Not in the Executive, for he only executes and cannot make the laws. Not in the Commander-in-Chief of the armies, for he can only hold them under military rule until the sovereign legislative power of the conqueror shall give them law. . . .

Members of Congress Must Work Together

Congress alone can do it. But Congress does not mean the Senate, or the House of Representatives, and President, all acting severally. Their joint action constitutes Congress. Hence a law of Congress must be passed before any new State can be admitted; or any dead one revived. Until then no member can be lawfully admitted into either House. Hence it appears with how little knowledge of constitutional law each branch is urged to admit members separately from these destroyed States. The provision that "each House shall be the judge of the elections, returns, and qualifications of its own members," has not the most distant bearing on this question. Congress must create States and declare when they are entitled to be represented. Then each House must judge whether the members presenting themselves from a recognized State possess the requisite qualifications of age, residence, and citizenship; and whether the election and returns are according to law. The Houses, separately, can judge of nothing else. It seems amazing that any man of legal education could give it any larger meaning.

Congress must create States and declare when they are entitled to be represented.

It is obvious from all this that the first duty of Congress is to pass a law declaring the condition of these outside or defunct States, and providing proper civil governments for them. Since the conquest they have been governed by martial law. Military rule is necessarily despotic, and ought not to exist longer than is absolutely necessary. As there are no symptoms that the people of these provinces will be prepared to participate in constitutional government for some years, I know of no arrangement so proper for them as territorial governments. There they can learn the principles of freedom and eat the fruit of foul rebellion. Under such governments, while electing members to the Territorial Legislatures, they will necessarily mingle with those to whom Congress shall extend the right of suffrage. In territories Congress fixes the qualifications of electors; and I know of no better place nor better occasion for the conquered rebels and the conqueror to practice justice to all men, and to accustom themselves to make and obey equal laws.

As these fallen rebels cannot at their option re-enter the heaven which they have disturbed, the garden of Eden which they have deserted, as flaming swords are set at the gates to secure their exclusion, it becomes important to the welfare of the nation to inquire when the doors shall be re-opened for their admission.

Constitutional Amendments Proposed

According to my judgment they ought never to be reorganized as capable of acting in the Union, or of being counted as valid States, until the Constitution shall have been so amended as to make it what its framers intended; and so as to secure perpetual ascendency to the party of the Union; and so as to render our republican government firm and stable forever. The first of those amendments is to change the basis of representation among the States, from Federal numbers to actual voters. Now all the colored freemen in the slave States, and three-fifths of the slaves, are represented, though none of them have votes. The States have nineteen representatives of colored slaves. If the slaves are now free then they can add, for the other two-fifths, thirteen more, making the slave representation thirty-two. I suppose the free blacks in those States will give at least five more, making the representation of non-voting people of color about thirty-seven. The whole number of representatives now from the slave States is seventy. Add the other two fifths and it will be eighty-eight.

It is obvious . . . that the first duty of Congress is to pass a law declaring the condition of these . . . defunct States, and providing proper civil governments for them.

If the amendment prevails, and those States withhold the right of suffrage from persons of color, it will deduct about thirty-seven, leaving them but forty-five. With the basis unchanged, the eighty-three Southern members, with the Democrats that will in the best time be elected from the North, will always give them a majority in Congress and in the Electoral College. They will at the very first election take possession of the White House and the halls of Congress. I need not depict the ruin that would follow. Assumption of the rebel debt or repudiation of the Federal debt would be sure to follow. The oppression of the freedmen; the re-amendment of their State constitutions, and the re-establishment of slavery would be the inevitable result. That they would scorn and disregard their present constitutions, forced upon them in the midst of martial law, would be both natural and just. No one who has any regard for freedom of elections can look upon those governments forced upon them in duress, with any favor. If they should grant the right of suffrage to persons of color, I think there would always be Union white men enough in the South, aided by the blacks, to divide the representation, and thus continue the Republican ascendency. If they should refuse to thus alter their election laws it would reduce the representatives of the late slave States to about forty-five and render them powerless for ever.

It is plain that this amendment must be consummated before the defunct States are admitted to be capable of State action, or it never can be.

The proposed amendment to allow Congress to lay a duty on exports is precisely in the same situation. Its importance cannot well be over-stated. It is very obvious that for many years the South will not pay much under our internal revenue laws. The only article on which we can raise any considerable amount is cotton. It will be grown largely at once. With ten cents a pound export duty it would be furnished cheaper to foreign markets than they could obtain it from any other parts of the world. The late war has shown that. Two million bales exported, at five hundred pounds to the bale, would yield $100,000,000. This seems to be the chief revenue we shall ever derive from the South. Besides, it would be a protection to that amount to our domestic manufactures. Other proposed amendments—to make all laws uniform; to prohibit the assumption of the rebel debt—are of vital importance, and the only thing that can prevent the combined forces of copperheads and secessionists from legislating against the interests of the Union whenever they may obtain an accidental majority.

Aiding the Newly Freed Blacks

But this is not all that we ought to do before these inveterate rebels are invited to participate in our legislation. We have turned, or are about to turn, loose four million slaves without a hut to shelter them or a cent in their pockets. The infernal laws of slavery have prevented them from acquiring an education, understanding the commonest laws of contract, or of managing the ordinary business of life. This Congress is bound to provide for them until they can take care of themselves. If we do not furnish them with homesteads from forfeited rebel property, and hedge them around with protective laws; if we leave them to the legislation of their late masters, we had better left them in bondage. Their condition would be worse than that of our prisoners at Andersonville. If we fail in this great duty now, when we have the power, we shall deserve and receive the execration of history and of all future ages.

Two things are of vital importance.

1. So to establish a principle that none of the rebel States shall be counted in any of the amendments of the Constitution until they are duly admitted into the family of States by the law-making power of their conqueror. For more than six months the amendment of the Constitution abolishing slavery has been ratified by the legislatures of three-fourths of the States that acted on its passage by Congress, and which had Legislatures, or which were States capable of acting, or required to act, on the question.

The infernal laws of slavery have prevented them [blacks] from acquiring an education . . . or of managing the ordinary business of life.

I take no account of the aggregation of white-washed rebels, who without any legal authority have assembled in the capitals of the late rebel States and simulated legislative bodies. Nor do I regard with any respect the cunning by-play into which they deluded the Secretary of State by frequent telegraphic announcements that "South Carolina had adopted the amendment;" "Alabama has adopted the amendment, being the twenty-seventh State;" etc. This was intended to delude the people, and accustom Congress to hear repeated the names of these extinct States as if they were alive; when, in truth, they have no more existence than the revolted cities of Latium, two-thirds of whose people were colonized and their property confiscated, and their right of citizenship withdrawn by conquering and avenging Rome.

2. It is equally important to the stability of this Republic that, it should now be solemnly decided what power can revive, re-create, and reinstate these provinces into the family of States, and invest them with the rights of American citizens. It is time that Congress should assent its sover-

eignty and assume something of the dignity of a Roman Senate. It is fortunate that the President invites Congress to take this manly attitude. After stating with great frankness in his able message his theory, which, however, is found to be impracticable, and which I believe very few now consider tenable, he refers the whole matter to the judgment of Congress. If Congress should fail firmly and wisely to discharge that high duty it is not the fault of the President.

Not a "White Man's Government"

This Congress owes it to its own character to set the seal of reprobation upon a doctrine which is becoming too fashionable, and unless rebuked will be the recognized principle of our Government. Governor [Benjamin F.] Perry [the appointed provisional governor of South Carolina] and other provisional governors and orators proclaim that "this is the white man's Government." The whole copperhead party, pondering to the lowest prejudices of the ignorant, repeat the cuckoo cry, "This is the white man's Government." Demagogues of all parties, even some high in authority, gravely shout, "This is the white man's Government." What is implied by this? That one race of men are to have the exclusive right forever to rule this nation, and to exercise all acts of sovereignty, while all other races and nations and colors are to be their subjects, and have no voice in making the laws and choosing the rulers by whom they are to be governed. Wherein does this differ from slavery except in degree? Does not this contradict all the distinctive principles of the Declaration of Independence? When the great and good men promulgated that instrument, and pledged their lives and sacred honors to defend it, it was supposed to form an epoch in civil government. Before that time it was held that the right to rule was vested in families, dynasties, or races, not because of superior intelligence or virtue, but because of a divine right to enjoy exclusive privileges.

Our fathers repudiated the whole doctrine of the legal superiority of families or races, and proclaimed the equality of men before the law. Upon that they created a revolution and built the Republic. They were prevented by slavery from perfecting the superstructure whose foundation they had thus broadly laid. For the sake of the Union they consented to wait, but never relinquished the idea of its final completion. The time to which they looked forward with anxiety has come. It is our duty to complete their work. If this republic is not now made to stand on their great principles, it has no honest foundation, and the Father of all men will still shake it to its centre. If we have not yet been sufficiently scourged for our national sin to teach us to do justice to all God's creatures, without distinction of race or color, we must expect the still more heavy vengeance of an offended Father, still increasing his inflictions as he increased the severity of the plagues of Egypt until the tyrant consented to do justice. And when that tyrant repented of his reluctant consent, and attempted to re-enslave the people, as our Southern tyrants are attempting to do now, he filled the Red sea with broken chariots and drowned horses, and strewed the shores with dead men's carcasses.

Mr. Chairman, I trust the Republican party will not be alarmed at what I am saying. I do not profess to speak their sentiments, nor must they be held responsible for them. I speak for myself, and take the responsibility, and will settle with my intelligent constituents.

This is not a "white man's Government," in the exclusive sense in which it is used. To say so is political blasphemy, for it violates the fundamental principles of our gospel of liberty. This is man's Government; the Government of all men alike; not that all men will have equal power and sway within it. Accidental circumstances, natural and acquired endowment and ability, will vary their fortunes. But equal rights to all the privileges of the Government is innate in every immortal being, no matter what the shape or color of the tabernacle which he inhabits.

If equal privileges were granted to all, I should not expect any but white men to be elected to office for long ages to come. The prejudice engendered by slavery would not soon permit merit to be preferred to color. But it would still be beneficial to the weaker races. In a country where political divisions will always exist, their power, joined with just white men, would greatly modify, if it did not entirely prevent, the injustice of majorities. Without the right of suffrage in the late slave States, (I do not speak of the free States,) I believe the slaves had far better been left in bondage. I see it stated that very distinguished advocates of the right of suffrage lately declared in this city that they do not expect to obtain it by Congressional legislation, but only by Administrative action, because, as one gallant gentleman said, the States had not been out of the Union. Then they will never get it. The President is far sounder than they. He sees that Administrative action has nothing to do with it. If it ever is to come, it must be by Constitutional amendments or Congressional action in the Territories, and in enabling acts.

How shameful that men of influence should mislead and miseducate the public mind! They proclaim, "This is the white man's Government," and the whole coil of copperheads echo the same sentiment, and upstart, jealous Republicans join the cry. Is it any wonder ignorant foreigners and illiterate natives should learn this doctrine, and be led to despise and maltreat a whole race of their fellow-men?

The South Should Not Be Treated as Conquered Territory

Andrew Johnson

Andrew Johnson, a Tennessee Democrat, was the only Southern senator to support the Union and not resign his seat during the Civil War. Selected to be Abraham Lincoln's running mate in the 1864 presidential election, Johnson became president when Lincoln was assassinated in April 1865.

By the time Johnson delivered the following State of the Union address to Congress in December 1867, he had spent almost two years enmeshed in a power struggle with Congress over Reconstruction. In 1866 and 1867 Congress passed numerous Reconstruction laws over his veto, dividing the Southern states into five military districts and mandating the establishment of new governments based on universal (male) suffrage. In his speech, Johnson argues that treating the South as conquered territory by placing it under direct federal military control is unconstitutional. He asserts that the Southern states have never been separated from the Union and cannot be denied their basic constitutional rights. In addition to pleas for fidelity to the U.S. Constitution, Johnson's arguments include warnings against giving blacks too much political power.

When a civil war has been brought to a close, it is manifestly the first interest and duty of the state to repair the injuries which the war has inflicted, and to secure the benefit of the lessons it teaches as fully and as speedily as pos-

Andrew Johnson, State of the Union address, December 3, 1867.

sible. This duty was, upon the termination of the rebellion, promptly accepted, not only by the executive department, but by the insurrectionary States themselves, and restoration in the first moment of peace was believed to be as easy and certain as it was indispensable. The expectations, however, then so reasonably and confidently entertained were disappointed by legislation from which I felt constrained by my obligations to the Constitution to withhold my assent.

It is clear to my apprehension that the States lately in rebellion are still members of the National Union.

It is therefore a source of profound regret that in complying with the obligation imposed upon the President by the Constitution to give to Congress from time to time information of the state of the Union I am unable to communicate any definitive adjustment, satisfactory to the American people, of the questions which since the close of the rebellion have agitated the public mind. On the contrary, candor compels me to declare that at this time there is no Union as our fathers understood the term, and as they meant it to be understood by us. The Union which they established can exist only where all the States are represented in both Houses of Congress; where one State is as free as another to regulate its internal concerns according to its own will, and where the laws of the central Government, strictly confined to matters of national jurisdiction, apply with equal force to all the people of every section. That such is not the present "state of the Union" is a melancholy fact, and we must all acknowledge that the restoration of the States to their proper legal relations with the Federal Government and with one another, according to the terms of the original compact, would be the greatest temporal blessing which God, in His kindest providence, could bestow upon this nation. It becomes our imperative duty to consider whether or not it is impossible to effect this most desirable consummation.

Applying the Constitution

The Union and the Constitution are inseparable. As long as one is obeyed by all parties, the other will be preserved; and if one is destroyed, both must perish together. The destruction of the Constitution will be followed by other and still greater calamities. It was ordained not only to form a more perfect union between the States, but to "establish justice, insure domestic tranquility, provide for the common defense, promote the general welfare, and secure the blessings of liberty to ourselves and our posterity." Nothing but implicit obedience to its requirements in all parts of the country will accomplish these great ends. Without that obedience we can look forward only to continual outrages upon individual rights, incessant breaches of the public peace, national weakness, financial dishonor, the total loss of our prosperity, the general corruption of morals, and the final extinction of popular freedom. To save our country from evils so appalling as these, we should renew our efforts again and again.

It can not be that a successful war, waged for the preservation of the Union, had the legal effect of dissolving it.

To me the process of restoration seems perfectly plain and simple. It consists merely in a faithful application of the Constitution and laws. The execution of the laws is not now obstructed or opposed by physical force. There is no military or other necessity, real or pretended, which can prevent obedience to the Constitution, either North or South. All the rights and all the obligations of States and individuals can be protected and enforced by means perfectly consistent with the fundamental law. The courts may be everywhere open, and if open their process would be unimpeded. Crimes against the United States can be prevented or punished by the proper judicial authorities in a manner entirely practicable and legal. There is therefore no reason why the Constitution should not be obeyed, unless those who exercise its powers have determined that it shall be disregarded and violated. The mere naked will of this Government, or of some one or more of its branches, is the only obstacle that can exist to a perfect union of all the States. . . .

It is clear to my apprehension that the States lately in rebellion are still members of the National Union. When did they cease to be so? The "ordinances of secession" adopted by a portion (in most of them a very small portion) of their citizens were mere nullities. If we admit now that they were valid and effectual for the purpose intended by their authors, we sweep from under our feet the whole ground upon which we justified the war. Were those States afterwards expelled from the Union by the war? The direct contrary was averred by this Government to be its purpose, and was so understood by all those who gave their blood and treasure to aid in its prosecution. It can not be that a successful war, waged for the preservation of the Union, had the legal effect of dissolving it. The victory of the nation's arms was not the disgrace of her policy; the defeat of secession on the battlefield was not the triumph of its lawless principle. Nor could Congress, with or without the consent of the Executive, do anything which would have the effect, directly or indirectly, of separating the States from each other. To dissolve the Union is to repeal the Constitution which holds it together, and that is a power which does not belong to any department of this Government, or to all of them united.

Treated as States

This is so plain that it has been acknowledged by all branches of the Federal Government. The Executive (my predecessor as well as myself) and the heads of all the Departments have uniformly acted upon the principle that the Union is not only undissolved, but indissoluble. Congress submitted an amendment of the Constitution to be ratified by the Southern States, and accepted their acts of ratification as a necessary and lawful exercise of their highest function. If they were not States, or were States out of the Union, their consent to a change in the fundamental law of the Union would have been nugatory, and Congress in asking it committed a political absurdity. The judiciary has also given the solemn sanction of its authority to the same view of the case. The judges of the Supreme Court have included the Southern States in their circuits, and they are constantly, *in banc* and elsewhere, exercising jurisdiction which does not belong to them unless those States are States of the Union.

If the Southern States are component parts of the Union, the Constitution is the supreme law for them, as it is for all the other States. They are bound to obey it, and so are we. The right of the Federal Government, which is clear and unquestionable, to enforce the Constitution upon them implies the correlative obligation on our part to observe its limitations and execute its guaranties. Without the Constitution we are nothing; by, through, and under the Constitution we are what it makes us. We may doubt the wisdom of the law, we may not approve of its provisions, but we can not violate it merely because it seems to confine our powers within limits narrower than we could wish. It is not a question of individual or class or sectional interest, much less of party predominance, but of duty—of high and sacred duty—which we are all sworn to perform. If we can not support the Constitution with the cheerful alacrity of those who love and believe in it, we must give to it as least the fidelity of public servants who act under solemn obligations and commands which they dare not disregard.

Andrew Johnson

The constitutional duty is not the only one which requires the States to be restored. There is another consideration which, though of minor importance, is yet of great weight. On the 22d day of July, 1861, Congress declared by an almost unanimous vote of both Houses that the war should be condemned solely for the purpose of preserving the Union and maintaining the supremacy of the Federal Constitution and laws, without impairing the dignity, equality, and rights of the States or of individuals, and that when this was done the war should cease. I do not say that this declaration is personally binding on those who joined in making it, any more than individual members of Congress are personally bound to pay a public debt created under a law for which they voted. But it was a solemn, public, official pledge of the national honor, and I can not imagine upon what grounds the repudiation of it is to be justified. If it be said that we are not bound to keep faith with rebels, let it be remembered that this promise was not made to rebels only. Thousands of true men in the South were drawn to our standard by it, and hundreds of thousands in the North gave their lives in the belief that it would be carried out. It was made on the day after the first great battle of the war had been fought and lost. All patriotic and intelligent men then saw the necessity of giving such an assurance, and believed that without it the war would end in disaster to our cause. Having given that assurance in the extremity of our peril, the violation of it now, in the day of our power, would be a rude rending of that good faith which holds the moral world together; our country would cease to have any claim upon the confidence of men; it would make the war not only a failure, but a fraud. . . .

Unjust Punishment

I have no desire to save from the proper and just consequences of their great crime those who engaged in rebellion against the Government, but as a mode of punishment the measures under consideration are the most unreasonable that could be invented. Many of those people are perfectly innocent; many kept their fidelity to the Union untainted to the last; many were incapable of any legal offense; a large proportion even of the persons able to bear arms were forced into rebellion against their will, and of those who are guilty with their own consent the degrees of guilt are as various as the shades of their character and temper. But these acts of Congress confound them all together in one common doom. Indiscriminate vengeance upon classes, sects, and parties, or upon whole communities, for offenses committed by a portion of them against the governments to which they owed obedience was common in the barbarous ages of the world; but Christianity and civilization have made such progress that recourse to a punishment so cruel and unjust would meet with the condemnation of all unprejudiced and right-minded men. The punitive justice of this age, and especially of this country, does not consist in stripping whole States of their liberties and reducing all their people, without distinction, to the condition of slavery. It deals separately with each individual, confines itself to the forms of law, and vindicates its own purity by an impartial examination of every case before a competent judicial tribunal. If this does not satisfy all our desires with regard to Southern rebels, let us console ourselves by reflecting that a free Constitution, triumphant in war and unbroken in peace, is worth far more to us and our children than the gratification of any present feeling.

I am aware it is assumed that this system of government for the Southern States is not to be perpetual. It is true this military government is to be only provisional, but it is through this temporary evil that a greater evil is to be made perpetual. If the guaranties of the Constitution can be broken provisionally to serve a temporary purpose, and in a part only of the country, we can destroy them everywhere and for all time. Arbitrary measures often change, but they generally change for the worse. It is the curse of despotism that it has no halting place. The intermitted exercise of its power brings no sense of security to its subjects, for they can never know what more they will be called to endure when its red right hand is armed to plague them again. Nor is it possible to conjecture how or where power, unrestrained by law, may seek its next victims. The States that are still free may be enslaved at any moment; for if the Constitution does not protect all, it protects none. . . .

Negro Suffrage

It is manifestly and avowedly the object of these [Radical Reconstruction] laws to confer upon negroes the privilege of voting and to disfranchise such a number of white citizens as will give the former a clear majority at all elections in the Southern States. This, to the minds of some persons, is so important that a violation of the Constitution is justified as a means of bringing it about. The morality is always false which excuses a wrong because it proposes to accomplish a desirable end. We are not permitted to do evil that good may come. But in this case the end itself is evil, as well as the means. The subjugation of the States to negro domination would be worse than the military despotism under which they are now suffering. It was believed beforehand that the people would endure any amount of military oppression for any length of time rather than degrade themselves by subjection to the negro race. Therefore they have been left without a choice. Negro suffrage was established by act of Congress, and the military officers were commanded to superintend the process of clothing the negro race with the political privileges torn from white men. . . .

I repeat the expression of my willingness to join in any plan within the scope of our constitutional authority which promises to better the condition of the negroes in the South, by encouraging them in industry, enlightening their minds, improving their morals, and giving protection to all their just rights as freedmen. But the transfer of our political inheritance to them would, in my opinion, be an abandonment of a duty which we owe alike to the memory of our fathers and the rights of our children.

The plan of putting the Southern States wholly and the General Government partially into the hands of negroes is proposed at a time peculiarly unpropitious. The foundations of society have been broken up by civil war. Industry must be reorganized, justice reestablished, public credit maintained, and order brought out of confusion. To accomplish these ends would require all the wisdom and virtue of the great men who formed our institutions originally. I confidently believe that their descendants will be equal to the arduous task before them, but it is worse than madness to expect that negroes will perform it for us. Certainly we ought not to ask their assistance till we despair of our own competency.

The great difference between the two races in physical, mental, and moral characteristics will prevent an amalgamation or fusion of them together in one homogeneous mass. If the inferior obtains the ascendency over the other, it will govern with reference only to its own interests—for it will recognize no common interest—and create such a tyranny as this continent has never yet witnessed. Already the negroes are influenced by promises of confiscation and plunder. They are taught to regard as an enemy every white man who has any respect for the rights of his own race. If this continues it must become worse and worse, until all order will be subverted, all industry cease, and the fertile fields of the South grow up into a wilderness. Of all the dangers which our nation has yet encountered, none are equal to those which must result from the success of the effort now making to Africanize the half of our country.

5

The Federal Government Must Act Against Ku Klux Klan Terrorism

Albion W. Tourgee

Albion W. Tourgee was one of the so-called "carpetbaggers"—white Northerners who settled in the South following the Civil War and became involved in local politics. Tourgee, a lawyer and Civil War veteran, moved to North Carolina and took part in writing that state's 1868 constitution. A leading and outspoken Republican, he served six years as a judge in North Carolina's state superior court.

The efforts of Tourgee and others to reconstruct Southern society were hampered by local resistance that sometimes was carried out by secret fraternities that engaged in vigilantism. The Ku Klux Klan, an order founded in Tennessee in 1866 whose members dressed in white robes, became the most famous of these groups. In an 1870 letter to North Carolina's Republican senator Joseph C. Abbott, Tourgee describes how Republican officeholders and supporters, along with blacks in general, are being victimized by violent and sometimes murderous attacks by the Ku Klux Klan and reports that victims of violence have no recourse with local governments or law enforcement. In his letter, which was published in the *New York Tribune*, Tourgee strongly criticizes the federal government for failing to take action to enforce law and order in the South.

Gen. Jos. C. Abbott—*My Dear General:* It is my mournful duty to inform you that our friend John W.

Albion W. Tourgee, *Some of the Outrages—Letter from Judge Tourgee to Senator Abbott*, Greensboro, NC, May 24, 1870.

Stephens, State Senator from Caswell, is dead. He was foully murdered by the Ku-Klux in the Grand Jury room of the Court House on Saturday or Saturday night last. The circumstances attending his murder have not yet fully come to light there. So far as I can learn, I judge these to have been the circumstances: He was one of the Justices of the Peace in that township, and was accustomed to hold court in that room on Saturdays. It is evident that he was set upon by some one while holding this court, or immediately after its close, and disabled by a sudden attack, otherwise there would have been a very sharp resistance, as he was a man, and always went armed to the teeth. He was stabbed five or six times, and then hanged on a hook in the Grand Jury room, where he was found on Sunday morning. Another brave, honest Republican citizen has met his fate at the hands of these fiends. Warned of his danger, and fully cognizant of the terrible risk which surrounded him, he still manfully refused to quit the field. Against the advice of his friends, against the entreaties of his family, he constantly refused to leave those who had stood by him in the day of his disgrace and peril. He was accustomed to say that 3,000 poor, ignorant, colored Republican voters in that county had stood by him and elected him, at the risk of persecution and starvation, and that he had no idea of abandoning them to the Ku-Klux. He was determined to stay with them, and either put an end to these outrages, or die with the other victims of Rebel hate and national apathy. . . . There have been twelve murders in five counties of the district during the past eighteen months, by bands of disguised villains. In addition to this, from the best information I can derive, I am of the opinion that in this district alone there have been 1,000 outrages of a less serious nature perpetrated by the same masked fiends. Of course this estimate is not made from any absolute record, nor is it possible to ascertain with accuracy the entire number of beatings and other outrages which have been perpetrated. The uselessness, the utter futility of complaint from the lack of ability in the laws to punish is fully known to all. The danger of making such complaint is also well understood. It is therefore not unfrequently by accident that the outrage is found out, and unquestionably it is frequently absolutely concealed. Thus, a respectable, hard working white carpenter was working for a neighbor, when accidentally his shirt was torn, and disclosed his back scarred and beaten. The poor fellow begged for the sake of his wife and children that nothing might be said about it, as the Ku-Klux had threatened to kill him if he disclosed how he had been outraged. Hundreds of cases have come to my notice and that of my solicitor. . . .

Crimes of the Klan

Men and women come scarred, mangled, and bruised, and say: "The Ku-Klux came to my house last night and beat me almost to death, and my old woman right smart, and shot into the house, 'bust' the door down, and told me they would kill me if I made complaint;" and the bloody mangled forms attest the truth of their declarations. On being asked if any one knew any of the party it will be ascertained that there was no recognition, or only the most uncertain and doubtful one. In such cases as these nothing can be done by the court. We have not been accustomed to enter them on record. A man of the best standing in Chatham told me that he could count up 200 and upward in that county. In Alamance County, a citizen in conversation one evening enumerated upward of 50 cases which had occurred within his own knowledge, and in one section of the county. He gave it as his opinion that there had been 200 cases in that county. I have no idea that he exceeded the proper estimate. That was six months ago, and I am satisfied that another hundred would not cover the work done in that time.

These crimes have been of every character imaginable. Perhaps the most usual has been the dragging of men and women from their beds, and beating their naked bodies with hickory switches, or as witnesses in an examination the other day said, "sticks" between a "switch" and a "club." From 50 to 100 blows is the usual allowance, sometimes 200 and 300 blows are administered. Occasionally an instrument of torture is owned. Thus in one case two women, one 74 years old, were taken out, stripped naked, and beaten with a paddle, with several holes bored through it. The paddle was about 30 inches long, 3 or 4 inches wide, and ¼ of an inch thick, of oak. Their bodies were so bruised and beaten that they were sickening to behold. They were white women and of good character until the younger was seduced, and swore her child to its father. Previous to that and so far as others were concerned her character was good.

Again, there is sometimes a fiendish malignity and cunning displayed in the form and character of the outrages. For instance, a colored man was placed astride of a log, and an iron staple driven through his person into the log. In another case, after a band of them had in turn violated a young negro girl, she was forced into bed with a colored man, their bodies were bound together face to face, and the fire from the hearth piled upon them. The K.K.K. rode off and left them, with shouts of laughter. Of course the bed was soon in flames, and somehow they managed to crawl out, though terribly burned and scarred. The house was burned.

Any member of Congress who . . . does not . . . urge immediate . . . and thorough measures to put an end to these outrages . . . is a coward, a traitor, or a fool.

I could give other incidents of cruelty, such as hanging up a boy of nine years old until he was nearly dead, to make him tell where his father was hidden, and beating an old negress of 103 years old with garden pallings because she would not own that she was afraid of the Ku-Klux. But it is unnecessary to go into further detail. In this district I estimate their offenses as follows, in the past ten months: Twelve murders, 9 rapes, 11 arsons, 7 mutilations, ascertained and most of them on record. In some no identification could be made.

Four thousand or 5,000 houses have been broken open, and property or persons taken out. In all cases all arms are taken and destroyed. Seven hundred or 800 persons have been beaten or otherwise maltreated. These of course are partly persons living in the houses which were broken into.

The Government Sleeps

And yet the Government sleeps. The poor disarmed nurses of the Republican party—those men by whose ballots the Republican party holds power—who took their lives in their hands when they cast their ballots for U.S. Grant and other officials—all of us who happen to be beyond the pale of the Governmental regard—must be sacrificed, murdered, scourged, mangled, because some contemptible party scheme might be foiled by doing us justice. I could stand it very well to fight for Uncle Sam, and was never known to refuse an invitation on such an occasion; but this lying down, tied hand and foot with the shackles of the law, to be killed by the very dregs of the rebellion, the scum of the earth, and not allowed either the consolation of fighting or the satisfaction that our "fall" will be noted by the Government, and protection given to others thereby, is somewhat too hard. I am ashamed of the nation that will let its citizens be slain by scores, and scourged by thousands, and offer no remedy or protection. I am ashamed of a State which has not sufficient strength to protect its own officers in the discharge of their duties, nor guarantee the safety of any man's domicile throughout its length and breadth. I am ashamed of a party which, with the reins of power in its hands, has not nerve or decision enough to arm its own adherents, or to protect them from assassinations at the hands of their opponents. A General who in time of war would permit 2,000 or 3,000 of his men to be bushwhacked and destroyed by private treachery even in an enemy's country without any one being punished for it would be worthy of universal execration, and would get it, too. How much more worthy of detestation is a Government which in time of peace will permit such wholesale slaughter of its citizens? It is simple cowardice, inertness, and wholesale demoralization. The wholesale slaughter of the war has dulled our Nation's sense of horror at the shedding of blood, and the habit of regarding the South as simply a laboratory, where every demagogue may carry on his reconstructionary experiments at will, and not as an integral party of the Nation itself, has led our Government to shut its eyes to the atrocities of these times. Unless these evils are speedily remedied, I tell you, General, the Republican party has signed its death warrant. It is a party of cowards or idiots—I don't care which alternative is chosen. The remedy is in our hands, and we are afraid or too dull to bestir ourselves and use it.

But you will tell me that Congress is ready and willing to act if it only knew what to do. Like the old Irish woman it wrings its hands and cries, "O Lawk, O Lawk; if I only knew which way." And yet this same Congress has the control of the militia and can organize its own force in every county in the United States, and arm more or less of it. This same Congress has the undoubted right to guarantee and provide a republican government, and protect every citizen in "life, liberty, and the pursuit of happiness," as well as the power conferred by the XVth Amendment. And yet we suffer and die in peace and murderers walk abroad with the blood yet fresh upon their garments, unharmed, unquestioned and unchecked. Fifty thousand dollars given to good detectives would secure, if well used, a complete knowledge of all this gigantic organization of murderers. In connection with an organized and armed militia, it would result in the apprehension of any number of these Thugs *en masque* and with blood on their hands. What then is the remedy? *First:* Let Congress give to the U.S. Courts, or to Courts of the States under its own laws, cognizance of this class of crimes, as crimes against the nation, and let it provide that this legislation be enforced. Why not, for instance, make going armed and masked or disguised, or masked or disguised in the night time, an act of insurrection or sedition? *Second:* Organize militia, National—State militia is a nuisance—and arm as many as may be necessary in each county to enforce its laws. *Third:* Put detectives at work to get hold of this whole organization. Its ultimate aim is unquestionably to revolutionize the Government. If we have not pluck enough for this, why then let us just offer our throats to the knife, emasculate ourselves, and be a nation of self-subjugated slaves at once.

A Personal Request

And now, Abbott, I have but one thing to say to you. I have very little doubt that I shall be one of the next victims. My steps have been dogged for months, and only a good opportunity has been wanting to secure to me the fate which Stephens has just met, and I speak earnestly upon this matter. I feel that I have a right to do so, and a right to be heard as well, and with this conviction I say to you plainly that any member of Congress who, especially if from the South, does not support, advocate, and urge immediate, active, and thorough measures to put an end to these outrages, and make citizenship a privilege, is a coward, a traitor, or a fool. The time for action has come, and the man who has now only speeches to make over some Constitutional scarecrow, deserves to be damned.

Chapter

Securing the Rights of Blacks

1

The Freedmen's Bureau Is Essential

Thomas Conway

Created by Congress in March 1865 to provide for the welfare of the newly freed slaves, the Freedmen's Bureau was an early focal point of contention regarding Reconstruction. In addition to dispensing food and medical care, its agents helped establish schools, brokered labor agreements between former slaves and owners, and in a few cases resettled freed slaves on confiscated land. Many white Southerners resented the bureau's presence. In 1866 President Andrew Johnson and Republicans in Congress debated whether to extend its life.

The following is taken from 1866 testimony before a special congressional committee by Thomas Conway, an Irish-born Baptist minister who was a Union army chaplain during the Civil War. Following the war he became a Freedmen's Bureau agent in Louisiana. Responding to questions by George H. Williams, a Republican senator from Oregon, Conway paints a bleak picture of race relations in Louisiana and asserts that the Freedmen's Bureau is necessary to shield blacks from violent retribution by local whites and attempts to impose a labor system resembling slavery. He also argues in favor of black suffrage and education.

▬▬▬▬▬▬▬▬▬▬▬▬▬▬▬▬▬▬▬▬▬▬▬▬▬▬▬▬▬▬▬▬▬▬▬▬▬▬

Question. What, in your judgment, would be the effect of the withdrawal of the Freedmen's Bureau or some organization or system like that from Louisiana?

Answer. I should expect in Louisiana, as in the whole southern country, that the withdrawal of the Freedmen's

Thomas Conway, *Reports of the Committees of the House of Representatives*, 39th Congress, 1st Session, February 22, 1866.

60

Bureau would be followed by a condition of anarchy and bloodshed, and I say that much in the light of as large an experience upon the subject as any man in the country. I have been in the army since the 19th of April, 1861; I have been over the whole country, almost from Baltimore to the Gulf. I was one of the first who held any official position in regard to the freedmen, and I am pained at the conviction I have in my own mind that if the Freedmen's Bureau is withdrawn the result will be fearful in the extreme. What it has already done and is now doing in shielding these people, only incites the bitterness of their foes. They will be murdered by wholesale, and they in their turn will defend themselves. It will not be persecution merely; it will be slaughter; and I doubt whether the world has ever known the like. These southern rebels, when the power is once in their hands, will stop with nothing short of extermination. Governor [James M.] Wells himself told me that he expected in ten years to see the whole colored race exterminated, and that conviction is shared very largely among the white people of the south. It has been threatened by leading men there that they would exterminate the freedmen. They have said so in my hearing. In reply I said that they could not drive the freedmen out of the nation, because, in the first place, they would not go; and for another reason, that they had no authority to drive them out; and for a third reason, that they were wanted in the south as laborers. To that they replied, that, if necessary, they would get their laborers from Europe; that white laborers would be more agreeable to them; that the negro must be gotten rid of in some way, and that, too, as speedily as possible. I have heard it so many times, and from so many different quarters, that I believe it is a fixed determination, and that they are looking anxiously to the extermination of the whole negro race from the country. There is an agent here now, with letters from the governor of Louisiana to parties in New York, with a view of entering at once upon negotiations to secure laborers from various parts of Europe. There are other parties endeavoring to get coolies into the south, and in various places there are immense efforts made to obtain white labor to supplant that of the negro. It is a part of the immense and desperate programme which they have adopted and expect to carry out within ten years. It is the same determination to which I referred in my report. I said the negro race would be extermi-

nated unless protected by the strong arm of the government; no weak arm will do. The very strongest arm of the
government is needed to shield them. The wicked work has
already commenced, and it could be shown that the policy
pursued by the government is construed by the rebels as not
being opposed to it. . . .

Question. Are the people there disposed to resort to personal violence or chastisement to compel the negroes to
work now?

Answer. They are so disposed in nearly every instance. A
resort to violence is the first thought that I have seen exhibited when freedmen did not act exactly to suit the employer.
The planters frequently came to me with requests (in fact, it
was almost daily) to be allowed to correct the laborers on
their own plantations. It is the universal conviction, and the
universal purpose with them, too, to do that so far as they
are allowed to do it; and, so far as they can, they will do it.
The only constraint put upon them in regard to it is
through the agency of the Freedmen's Bureau. Without
that, I am satisfied, they would very rapidly return to the old
system of slavery. In some portions of the State of
Louisiana, now, they have organized patrols of militiamen,
who go up and down the roads the same as if they were
scouting in time of war, to prevent the negroes from going
from one place to another. I am satisfied, from the most re-
liable reports, that under the most strict rules of evidence it
could be proved that in portions of the State these acts are
being done the same as under the old system; that, except as
regards buying and selling, the old system of slavery is being carried on in all its essential features, and that there is a
deep-rooted determination, arising from the old habits of
treating the negro, to continue the same treatment and the
same restrictions that existed prior to the war. . . .

Question. What is your opinion as to the extent of general knowledge among the freedmen; and what is their capacity for understanding their rights and the questions that
are being agitated in the country?

Answer. I have taken a great deal of pains to secure, for
my own satisfaction, accurate information on that subject,
and I have questioned the lowest and meanest of them as to
their ideas of liberty and their duty as citizens; and I have
never yet found any view expressed by them, or any evidence through their answers or conduct, which led me to

think they were any lower or more ignorant than the lower order of the white people who live down there or that they had any less accurate knowledge of government and duty toward it than the lower class of white people. I have seen very ignorant white people there who had all the privileges of citizenship. I have seen them go to the polls and vote, when they had no better idea of the questions at issue in the election, or the importance of the act they were performing, than the lowest negro I ever saw. The great majority of colored people understand very well and have a very accurate idea of what their personal liberty is, and how far it is to be regulated in order to be a blessing to them, and a very good idea of their duty as citizens. They have one idea which underlies every other, and that is, that notwithstanding the treatment they receive at the hands of the government, and the want of complete protection and complete liberty the government has so far caused them to suffer, they believe that it will yet secure them full protection, full liberty, and a full enjoyment of all their rights as citizens and as men; and they are working very energetically in Louisiana for the attainment of that purpose. They have their societies and clubs, in which they canvass very carefully every act of the government in regard to them, and in regard to the rebels who live all around them. They read the newspapers pretty generally. I believe two-thirds of the negroes in Louisiana can read. They publish a newspaper there, read it, and sustain it. With the use of schools, and the diligence in learning among them, which arises partly from the suddenness of the opportunity presented, and in part from a desire to ascertain precisely what the government is doing for them, and how they can best live as men and citizens ought to live. These reasons, I think, mainly explain the causes of the desire they manifest in this regard, and the result will, I think, be their nearly all becoming quite intelligent in a short time.

The Right to Vote

Question. What, in your opinion, would be the effect upon whites, blacks, and all concerned, of giving the negro the right to vote?

Answer. I do not think the effect would be to inaugurate a war of races there, for this reason: The negroes are so numerous, and they would be so intensely determined to enjoy what rights they have in that respect, that the whites would submit, seeing the impossibility of preventing it, and for the purpose of avoiding collisions and bloodshed in the country. The lives and safety of loyal white men require the protection and assistance that would grow from the negro's vote. I think the troops should be retained, and that small squads of them should be stationed all through the country, so as to shield the freedmen in the enjoyment of this right till the whites have become familiar with it. The militia forces should not be organized in the south during this generation. These things being done, my judgment is that there would be no trouble at all. On the contrary, it would, in a more speedy and thorough manner than any other, secure permanent peace and prosperity to the country. In the present condition of things there they cannot hope for peace or prosperity, because loyal men cannot remain without the protection of the government, and the negroes have no safety in the protection of their white foes. When the negroes come to see that their own life and liberty are to be sacrificed, they will struggle manfully against such a result, and they will importune the government, and call upon mankind to be their witness, until liberty and safety are insured them; they will persevere devotedly until their rights are accomplished. There are so many of them, and so many white people to help them, I don't see how the government can resist giving them every protection warranted by the Constitution.

2

The Freedmen's Bureau Is Harmful

James D.B. De Bow

The Freedmen's Bureau was created in March 1865 by Congress; its responsibilities included supervising the education and labor arrangements of former slaves. The following criticisms of the federal agency come from James D.B. De Bow, who was testifying on conditions in the South before Congress's Joint Committee on Reconstruction. De Bow, a publisher of a commercial and agricultural journal prior to the Civil War, was one of several ex-Confederate officials invited to present his views before Congress. He argues that interference by the Freedmen's Bureau has worsened relations between slaves and their former masters. His unfavorable opinions of the bureau and of blacks in general were representative of many whites in the South. De Bow's questioner was George H. Williams, a Republican senator from Oregon.

Question. What are the views and feelings of the people there as to the late war and its results, and as to the future condition of that State [Louisiana] in its relations to the federal government?

Answer. There seems to be a general—you may say universal—acquiescence in the results. There is a great deal of dissatisfaction as to the course in reference to their condition pursued by the federal government. I think the people having fairly tried the experiment of secession are perfectly satisfied with the result, and that there is no disposition in any quarter, in any shape or form, to embarrass the United

James D.B. De Bow, *Reports of the Committees of the House of Representatives*, 39th Congress, 1st Session, March 28, 1866.

States government, or to refrain from the most complete performance of all the duties of citizenship. I saw nothing of that sort. All parties, those who were opposed to the war and those who were in favor of the war, are now agreed that it is for the best interest of the State to perform all the duties of citizenship, and to accept whatever the government has effected in reference to the negro, as well as in reference to other questions. . . .

The Freedmen's Bureau, or any agency to interfere between the freedman and his former master, is only productive of mischief.

Question. What is your opinion of the necessity or utility of the Freedmen's Bureau, or of any agency of that kind?

Answer. I think if the whole regulation of the negroes, or freedmen, were left to the people of the communities in which they live, it will be administered for the best interest of the negroes as well as of the white men. I think there is a kindly feeling on the part of the planters towards the freedmen. They are not held at all responsible for anything that has happened. They are looked upon as the innocent cause. In talking with a number of planters, I remember some of them telling me they were succeeding very well with their freedmen, having got a preacher to preach to them and a teacher to teach them, believing it was for the interest of the planter to make the negro feel reconciled; for, to lose his services as a laborer for even a few months would be very disastrous. The sentiment prevailing is, that it is for the interest of the employer to teach the negro, to educate his children, to provide a preacher for him, and to attend to his physical wants. And I may say I have not seen any exception to that feeling in the south. Leave the people to themselves, and they will manage very well. The Freedmen's Bureau, or any agency to interfere between the freedman and his former master, is only productive of mischief. There are constant appeals from one to the other and continual annoyances. It has a tendency to create dissatisfaction and disaffection on the part of the laborer, and is in every respect in its result most unfavorable to the system of industry that is now being organized under the new order of things in the south. I do not think there is any difference of opinion upon this subject.

Question. Do you think the white men of the south would do justice by the negroes in making contracts and in paying them for their labor?

Answer. Before these negroes were freed, there were some two or three hundred thousand free negroes in the south, and some four or five hundred thousand of them in the country. There were a great many in Louisiana. There were in New Orleans some free negroes among the wealthiest men we had. I made a comparison when I was superintendent of the United States census in 1850, and found that the condition of the free negroes in the south, their education, &c., was better; that as a class they were immeasurably better off than the free people of the north. I never heard any cause of complaint of our treatment of these people in the south before the war, even from northern sources, and I do not presume there would be more cause of complaint now. If we performed our duty to this same class of population when the great mass of negroes were held by us as slaves, I think it should go very far to indicate that we should not be lacking in our duties to them now. There are free negroes in Louisiana who owned fifty or a hundred slaves, and plantations on the coast, and there were hundreds of them who owned more or less property.

Slavery vs. Free Labor

Question. What is your opinion as to the relative advantages to the blacks of the present system of free labor, as compared with that of slavery as it heretofore existed in this country?

Answer. If the negro would work, the present system is much cheaper. If we can get the same amount of labor from the same persons, there is no doubt of the result in respect to *economy*. Whether the same amount of labor can be obtained, it is too soon yet to decide. We must allow one summer to pass first. They are working now very well on the plantations. That is the general testimony. The negro women are not disposed to field work as they formerly were, and I think there will be less work from them in the future than there has been in the past. The men are rather inclined to get their wives into other employment, and I think that will be the constant tendency, just as it is with the whites. Therefore, the real number of agricultural laborers will be reduced. I have no idea if the efficiency of those who work will be increased. If we can only keep up their efficiency to the standard before the war, it will be better for the south, without doubt, upon the mere money question, because it is cheaper to hire the negro than to own him. Now a plantation can be worked without any outlay of capital by hiring the negro and hiring the plantation. . . .

Civil Rights and Education

Question. What do you find the disposition of the people as to the extension of civil rights to the blacks—the right to sue and enforce their contracts and to hold property, real and personal, like white people?

Answer. I think there is a willingness to give them every right except the right of suffrage. It is believed they are unfit to exercise that. The idea is entertained by many that they will eventually be endowed with that right. It is only a question of time; but the universal conviction is that if it ever be conceded, it will be necessary to prepare for it by slow and regular means, as the white race was prepared. I believe everybody unites in the belief that it would be disastrous to give the right of suffrage now. Time and circumstances may alter the case. There is no difference of opinion upon this subject now.

3

Black Suffrage Is the Key to Successful Reconstruction

Frederick Douglass

The following essay by noted black abolitionist Frederick Douglass was first published in *The Atlantic Monthly* in December 1866. By then Congress had passed some Reconstruction measures over President Johnson's veto, including extending the life of the Freedmen's Bureau and the 1866 Civil Rights Act. Douglass argues that such measures are not enough. The federal government cannot by itself protect the civil rights of blacks without becoming too powerful and despotic itself, he contends. State and local governments must instead take the lead in reconstructing the South and securing the rights of blacks. These governments will only be compelled to take such actions, he insists, if black men have the right to vote and thus have a say in government.

Frederick Douglass was at this time perhaps the most celebrated ex-slave in America. Having successfully escaped from slavery in 1838, he gained international renown as an abolitionist speaker and political activist. Unlike some abolitionists, he continued to press for suffrage and full civil rights for blacks after the Civil War.

The assembling of the Second Session of the Thirty-ninth Congress may very properly be made the occasion of a few earnest words on the already much-worn topic of reconstruction.

Frederick Douglass, "Reconstruction," *The Atlantic Monthly*, December 1866.

Seldom has any legislative body been the subject of a solicitude more intense, or of aspirations more sincere and ardent. There are the best of reasons for this profound interest. Questions of vast moment, left undecided by the last session of Congress, must be manfully grappled with by this. No political skirmishing will avail. The occasion demands statesmanship.

The arm of the Federal government is long, but it is far too short to protect the rights of individuals in the interior of distant States.

Whether the tremendous war so heroically fought and so victoriously ended shall pass into history a miserable failure, barren of permanent results,—a scandalous and shocking waste of blood and treasure,—a strife for empire, as [British foreign secretary] Earl [John] Russell characterized it, of no value to liberty or civilization,—an attempt to reestablish a Union by force, which must be the merest mockery of a Union,—an effort to bring under Federal authority States into which no loyal man from the North may safely enter, and to bring men into the national councils who deliberate with daggers and vote with revolvers, and who do not even conceal their deadly hate of the country that conquered them; or whether, on the other hand, we shall, as the rightful reward of victory over treason have a solid nation, entirely delivered from all contradictions and social antagonisms, based upon loyalty, liberty, and equality, must be determined one way or the other by the present session of Congress. The last session really did nothing which can be considered final as to these questions. The Civil Rights Bill and the Freedmen's Bureau Bill and the proposed constitutional amendments, with the amendment already adopted and recognized as the law of the land, do not reach the difficulty, and cannot, unless the whole structure of the government is changed from a government by States to something like a despotic central government, with power to control even the municipal regulations of States, and to make them conform to its own despotic will. While there remains such an idea as the right of each State to control its own local affairs,—an idea, by the way, more deeply rooted in the minds of men of all sections of the country than perhaps any one other political idea,—no general assertion of human rights can be of any practical value. To change the character of the government at this point is neither possible nor desirable. All that is necessary to be done is to make the government consistent with itself, and render the rights of the States compatible with the sacred rights of human nature.

The arm of the Federal government is long, but it is far too short to protect the rights of individuals in the interior of distant States. They must have the power to protect themselves, or they will go unprotected, in spite of all the laws the Federal government can put upon the national statute-book.

Every Citizen Must Have the Franchise

Slavery, like all other great systems of wrong, founded in the depths of human selfishness, and existing for ages, has not neglected its own conservation. It has steadily exerted an influence upon all around it favorable to its own continuance. And today it is so strong that it could exist, not only without law, but even against law. Custom, manners, morals, religion, are all on its side everywhere in the South; and when you add the ignorance and servility of the ex-slave to the intelligence and accustomed authority of the master, you have the conditions, not out of which slavery will again grow, but under which it is impossible for the Federal government to wholly destroy it, unless the Federal government be armed with despotic power, to blot out State authority, and to station a Federal officer at every cross-road. This, of course, cannot be done, and ought not even if it could. The true way and the easiest way is to make our government entirely consistent with itself, and give to every loyal citizen the elective franchise,—a right and power which will be ever present, and will form a wall of fire for his protection.

The people themselves demand such a reconstruction as shall put an end to the present anarchical state of things in the late rebellious States.

One of the invaluable compensations of the late rebellion is the highly instructive disclosure it made of the true source of danger to republican government. Whatever may be tolerated in monarchical and despotic governments, no republic is safe that tolerates a privileged class, or denies to any of its citizens equal rights and equal means to maintain them.

It remains now to be seen whether we have the needed courage to have that cause [for rebellion] entirely removed from the Republic. At any rate, to this grand work of national regeneration and entire purification Congress must now address itself, with full purpose that the work shall this time be thoroughly done.

If time was at first needed, Congress has now had time. All the requisite materials from which to form an intelligent judgment are now before it. Whether its members look at the origin, the progress, the termination of the war, or at the mockery of a peace now existing, they will find only one unbroken chain of argument in favor of a radical policy of reconstruction.

Reconstruction by the People

The people themselves demand such a reconstruction as shall put an end to the present anarchical state of things in the late rebellious States,—where frightful murders and wholesale massacres are perpetrated in the very presence of Federal soldiers. This horrible business they require shall cease. They want a reconstruction such as will protect loyal men, black and white, in their persons and property: such a one as will cause Northern industry, Northern capital, and Northern civilization to flow into the South, and make a man from New England as much at home in Carolina as elsewhere in the Republic. No Chinese wall can now be tolerated. The South must be opened to the light of law and liberty, and this session of Congress is relied upon to accomplish this important work.

The plain, common-sense way of doing this work is simply to establish in the South one law, one government, one administration of justice, one condition to the exercise of the elective franchise, for men of all races and colors alike. This great measure is sought as earnestly by loyal white men as by loyal blacks, and is needed alike by both. Let sound political prescience but take the place of an unreasoning prejudice, and this will be done.

4

A Federal Civil Rights Bill Is Dangerous

Robert B. Vance

Congress debated and passed two major laws dealing with the civil rights of blacks during Reconstruction. The Civil Rights Act of 1866 granted U.S. citizenship for African Americans and forbade states from discriminating on the basis of race (its principles were later enshrined in the Fourteenth Amendment to the Constitution, ratified in 1868). In 1870 Republican senator Charles Sumner introduced a second civil rights bill that was designed to ban racial segregation in schools and public facilities. The following is taken from an 1874 speech by one of the bill's opponents in Congress, Robert B. Vance. Vance, a former Civil War Confederate officer, served as a Democratic representative from North Carolina from 1873 to 1885. In his speech, he professes personal concern for blacks and argues that a new federal civil rights law would jeopardize peaceful race relations in the South.

M r. Speaker, having been unable to obtain the floor on the civil-rights bill, I propose to devote a portion of my time to the discussion of that subject; and I think I can do so without prejudice and without subjecting myself truthfully to the charge of hatred toward the colored race. In the will of my grandfather (who was one of those who struggled for liberty upon the heights of King's Mountain) he enjoined it upon his children and his grandchildren to treat kindly the colored people upon the plantation. I hope never to forget a sentiment so noble and so worthy of obe-

Robert B. Vance, *Congressional Record*, 43rd Congress, 1st Session, January 10, 1874.

dience. In fact, as a southern man, as one who has sympa-
thized from my earliest time of knowledge with the South
in all the great principles and struggles which have interested her, I have felt it my duty to advance in every laudable
way the interests of the colored race in this country. I have
even taught a colored Sunday-school of one hundred and
fifty scholars. I have endeavored in every way possible to advance the interests of that race. I feel, therefore, that I can
speak upon this subject without prejudice.

Unfounded Charges of Prejudice

The charge has been made against the people of the South
that their opposition to such measures as the civil-rights bill
has arisen from prejudice and hatred. This charge is unfounded; it is untrue. Before the war—in the days past and
gone—in the days when there were four million slaves in
the South, the churches of the South sent missionaries into
the cotton plantations, and down into the orange groves,
and out upon the rolling prairies of Texas. Into all parts of
the country where great numbers of colored people were
collected the churches sent their missionaries, and held up
there the standard of the Cross, instructing them in the sublime principles which relate to questions vastly more important than mere earthly things.

---

*The charge has been made against the people of
the South that their opposition to such measures
as the civil-rights bill has arisen from prejudice.
. . . This charge is unfounded.*

I have yet to meet the southern man (and I thank God
for it) who does not in his heart rejoice that the colored man
is free. In my intercourse with the people of my own land,
in my travels through the "sunny South," I have found the
feeling everywhere one of gratitude and thankfulness that
the chains of the colored man have been broken; that he is
now permitted to walk the earth a free man.

Sir, the people of the South were not to blame for the
introduction of slavery among them. It came from elsewhere, and became incorporated as a part of our institutions. The old colored women nursed the white children of

the South, while kindness and friendship were maintained between the two races. Such an institution could not be readily abolished. It could probably only be done by the shock of arms.

Every southern man who will call to mind the fact that after the thunder of artillery had ceased, when the clang of arms was no more heard in the country, the southern people rallied and took the oath to support the proclamations of Mr. Lincoln, in order that the colored man might be free. Those proclamations, Mr. Speaker, were regarded at the time as unconstitutional; yet the southern people were willing that the colored man should enjoy his freedom, and all over the South they came forward and took the oath to support those proclamations.

The real objection . . . to civil rights, so called, is that . . . it will be detrimental to the interests of both races.

Following hard upon that, the conventions of the Southern States assembled, and by a solemn act ratified the freedom of the colored man, confirming it forever by statute upon the records of their governments.

What else did they do? They went to work and secured the colored man in all his civil rights, or what may properly be termed civil rights. The people there consented that he should vote; they consented he should hold office; they consented he should serve upon juries; they consented that he should hold property, and that he should be a witness in court. All the real rights properly known as civil rights were guaranteed to the colored man in that section; and the charge cannot justly be made against this people that they are opposed to according civil rights to the colored man on account of any prejudice or hatred, for it is not in their hearts.

Civil Rights and Social Rights

Why, then, do we oppose the civil-rights bill? That is the question; and speaking as I do, and feeling as I speak, without prejudice, I will show what is the real objection to the bill known as the civil-rights bill. I think gentlemen of the House will bear me out when I say the title of the bill we had before us ought to be changed, and made to read thus:

"A bill to protect the colored people in their social rights." That is the way it should read.

Now, Mr. Speaker the distinguished gentleman from Massachusetts [Benjamin Butler] laid down the law, and it has not been controverted, that all men are entitled under the law to the right to go to a hotel, to ride in a public railway carriage, to interment, and to be taught in the public schools sustained by moneys raised by taxation.

It is laid down as the common law of the land. Now, let us see for a few minutes, Mr. Speaker, how the case stands. There is no railway car in all the South which the colored man cannot ride in. That is his civil right. This bill proposes that he should have the opportunity or the right to go into a first-class car and sit with white gentlemen and white ladies. I submit if that is not a social right. There is a distinction between the two. Now, there is not a hotel in the South where the colored man cannot get entertainment such as food and lodgings. That is his civil right. The bill of the committee provides that there shall be no distinction. Even if he is allowed to go into the dining-room, and is placed at a separate table because of his color, it will be a violation of this law. Placing him, therefore, at the same table with the whites is a social right.

It is a plain, simple truth, that in . . . having mixed schools you destroy the school system of the South.

Now, sir, provision has been made for free schools in my own native State of North Carolina. We have cheerfully taxed ourselves there for the education of our people, including the colored race; but separate schools are organized for the instruction of the latter. One of the civil rights of the colored man undoubtedly is the right to be educated out of moneys raised by taxation. His children, under the law, have that right; but this bill goes further, and provides that colored children shall go into the same school with white children, mixing the colored children and the white children in the same schools. I submit to the House whether that is not a social right instead of a civil right. Therefore it is I say this bill ought to be changed, or rather its title ought to be changed. The real objection, then, to civil rights, so called, is that it is not best for both races, that in fact it will be detrimental to the interests of both races.

Harmful Coercion

Now, Mr. Speaker, I propose to show briefly how that will be. In the first place, the true policy in regard to the intercourse of mankind all over this broad earth is in the recognition of the fact that such intercourse is one made up of mutual interests. It is the interest of the hotel-keeper to entertain his guests, it is the interest of the railway company to transport passengers; the interests are mutual; and that is the true policy all the world over. But whenever you undertake to force persons of color into their social rights, then, in my judgment, you have done the colored man a serious damage. Let the people of the South alone, sir, and this thing will adjust itself. It will come out all right. In coming to this city the other day colored men were sitting in first-class cars with their wives, where they were admitted by the managers of the road; and I am told in this city one of the first hotels admits colored men as guests. It will adjust itself if let alone; but if you undertake to coerce society before it is ready, you will damage the colored man in all his interests, and at the same time do damage to the white race.

There are between four and five millions of colored people in the South, whose interests are intimately and closely connected with those of the white people. The one cannot well do without the other. Where does the colored man get his place to live, where does he obtain employment? In a great measure from the white men of the country, and almost entirely from those opposed to this bill. And I tell the House now, through you, Mr. Speaker, that the great majority of the people of the Southern States, of all political shades of opinion, are opposed to anything like force in this matter.

Look at my own State, sir. As I went home from the capital during the holidays I met with republican members of the Legislature of North Carolina who stated that we ought to oppose this bill. Republicans do not want it. They think it is wrong. A resolution was introduced into the Legislature of North Carolina in regard to this subject, and it received a very small vote. It did not receive the vote of the republican party. And, sir, it is my opinion that the colored people of the South *en masse* do not want it. They do not want to be brought into apparent antagonism to the white people, because their interests are closely connected together. The colored man cannot do well in the South, he cannot prosper, unless he has the sympathies, unless he has the fostering hand, unless he has the kind care, of the white man extended to him; his interests will suffer if this should not be the case.

And, sir, it is necessary anyhow in this world of ours that there should be kindness running from heart to heart. There has been enough trouble and enough sorrow in this world already. War has stamped its foot upon human sympathies. It has left its scars upon every human heart, sir; and now there ought to be sympathy, there ought to be kindness, there ought to be oneness of interest pervading the whole land. And these people need that thing. You rob the colored man by the passage of this bill more or less of the friendship of the owners of the soil in the South. And you rob him, sir, of the opportunity of education. Gentlemen may treat this statement lightly. The distinguished gentleman from Massachusetts said the other day that he would not act under a threat. He regarded the declaration made here that the schools would be broken up as a threat. It was not a threat, sir, it is a solemn fact.

I ask the attention of the House to this fact: the University of South Carolina was one of the most honored in all the land. That university has turned out some of the most eminent men of this country—Presidents, Senators, governors, and distinguished military chieftains. Where, sir, is it now? In what condition is the University of South Carolina? A law was passed in South Carolina that colored students should be received into that institution. What has been the effect? Some time since there were only from six to nine scholars in the University of South Carolina; while the professors are paid out of moneys raised from the people by taxation. This is no threat, sir. It is a plain, simple truth, that in passing bills of this kind and having mixed schools you destroy the school system of the South. That is to be the effect; and you thereby lessen the chances of the colored children for an education.

Racial Antagonisms

There is another point to which I ask the attention of the House. A bill like this gives rise to an antagonism of races. If the people are let alone in the South they will adjust these things and there will be peace in the country. But by passing a bill of this kind you place a dangerous power in the hands of the vicious. Here comes a vicious colored man and presents himself at a hotel and demands that he be permitted to go to the table with the whites, and that he shall have his choice of rooms. The hotel-keeper, acting upon his right as he understands it, handed down from all ages, that "every man's house is his castle;" that no man can come into his house without his consent, recognizing that as being the old Anglo-Saxon law of our ancestors, may refuse. Then you have it placed in the power of this man to have the hotel-keeper arrested, tried, and fined a sum not less than $100 no more than $5,000. And that, sir, would be placing a dangerous power in the hands of the vicious.

It is absurd . . . to talk about the equality of the races.

This bill, Mr. Speaker, will, more or less, bring about an antagonism of the races; and that state of things would not be best for the colored man. I submit it in good faith, that if the question is ever presented in the South, shall this country be ruled by white men or ruled by colored men? the colored man is not able to stand any such an antagonism as that; he will necessarily, sir, go down. I ask what race has ever been able to stand before the Caucasian? Look at the history of the world. Where is the Indian? Why, sir, less than two centuries ago on this spot the Indian reared his wigwam and stood upon these hills and looked upon the broad, beautiful Potomac, or his eye swept over the hunting grounds of the West; and he had the title to this magnificent country. Where is he now? He has gone back, step by step, before the advancing march of the white man. No race, sir, in the world has been able to stand before the pure Caucasian. An antagonism of races will not be good for the colored man.

There is another objection to this bill. It begets hopes and raises an ambition in the minds of the colored man that can never be realized. It is true, sir, that we can find some ten or twelve members of Congress here from densely-populated regions of the South where the colored race is dominant. But how is it in other States? Where is the colored man from Massachusetts? Is he here? Where is even Fred Douglass, who is acknowledged to be a man of ability? Is he here? No, sir; he has not found his way into this House. This bill, therefore, as I have said, begets in the minds of these people hopes and an ambition that can never be realized; and in that view of the case it is unfortunate for them. And I say, sir, that it is not for the best interest of the white race that this bill should pass. And why? Because if the common schools are to be destroyed, which are beneficial to the colored man, their destruction will also be against the interests of the whites, and the poor white children of the South will fail to receive those educational advantages which they ought to have; and in that respect it will not be best for the white race.

Another view of this question, Mr. Speaker, is this: that by placing the colored race and the white race continually together, by throwing them into social contact, the result will be more or less that the distinction between them will be broken down, and that miscegenation and an admixture of the races will follow. Sir, it must necessarily follow on such close intercommunication. I presume that no man will stand upon this floor and say that it is best for all the races of men on the face of the earth to become one by amalgamation.

Let us look for a moment and see how it is. We are told that colored men have not succeeded in this country because they had been borne down by chains and slavery. I admit, sir, that the colored man when in a state of servitude had not much opportunity to develop his mind and expand the powers that God has given him; but will any gentleman on this floor undertake to say that the colored race has not had an equal chance in the world with the white race? I suppose no man will controvert the theory that colored men were at the tower of Babel, and that when God confounded the languages of men and sent them forth into the world the colored race was among them. Some went one way and some went another. Some went north and some south, some east and some west; they went into all portions of the world. Well, sir, what has been the history of the Caucasian race? It has gone on progressing; it has whitened every ocean on the globe with the sails of commerce; it has reared monuments which will be everlasting; it has stamped its language on the world—the strong German, the elegant French, the soft Italian, and the ever-living and ever-spoken English.

What language has the colored man given to the world? He started on an equal footing with the white race—what has he done? Look at Africa. There she is, bowed down by superstition and under the shadow of death.

Sir, it is absurd for gentlemen to talk about the equality of the races. But let us give to the colored man the opportunity of improvement; let us give him an education. I for one will vote cheerfully and gladly for the appropriation of a portion of the proceeds of the splendid domain of this country for the education of the colored race; but I think it ought to be done in separate schools. Sir, we have already given him the opportunity to be educated; we have allowed him to hold office; we have seen and heard colored men on this floor; they are here now.

I Would Not Beg

The bill ought not to pass; the matter ought to be left to the States. I will not undertake to argue the constitutionality of this question; that has been done by others, and well done. I have only spoken to the effect of the passage of such a measure, and what is best for the interests of both races; and I submit in concluding my remarks that we have really extended to the colored man everything that I think he ought to ask at our hands. If I belonged to the colored race I would not stand here and ask the passage of a law to force me into what are termed my civil rights. If I belonged to the colored race I would come up by my own merit. I would wait for time and opportunity, and I would not ask any help from Congress. I would not stand here as a beggar asking for these social rights; I would depend on my own merits.

5

A Federal Civil Rights Bill Is Necessary

Richard H. Cain

In 1874 Congress was debating a federal civil rights bill, originally introduced by Senator Charles Sumner, that called for racial integration of public schools and facilities. Richard H. Cain, one of sixteen African Americans elected to Congress during Reconstruction, spoke before Congress in January 1874 in support of the bill and to respond to one of its critics, Robert B. Vance. He argues that blacks should have the full protection of their civil rights based on the U.S. Constitution and its Fourteenth and Fifteenth Amendments.

A weakened version of Sumner's bill (permitting segregated schools) was passed in 1875, but was declared unconstitutional by the Supreme Court eight years later.

Cain, a minister for the African Methodist Episcopal Church, served as a South Carolina state senator from 1868 to 1872 and as a representative in Congress from 1873 to 1875 and again from 1877 to 1879.

Mr. Speaker, I feel called upon more particularly by the remarks of the gentleman from North Carolina [Robert B. Vance] on civil rights to express my views. For a number of days this question has been discussed, and various have been the opinions expressed as to whether or not the pending bill should be passed in its present form or whether it should be modified to meet the objections entertained by a number of gentlemen whose duty it will be to give their votes for or against its passage. It has been as-

Richard H. Cain, *Congressional Record*, 43rd Congress, 1st Session, January 10, 1874.

sumed that to pass this bill in its present form Congress would manifest a tendency to override the Constitution of the country and violate the rights of the States.

Whether it be true or false is yet to be seen. I take it, so far as the constitutional question is concerned, if the colored people under the law, under the amendments to the Constitution, have become invested with all the rights of citizenship, then they carry with them all rights and immunities accruing to and belonging to a citizen of the United States. If four, or nearly five, million people have been lifted from the thralldom of slavery and made free; if the Government by its amendments to the Constitution has guaranteed to them all rights and immunities, as to other citizens, they must necessarily therefore carry along with them all the privileges enjoyed by all other citizens of the Republic.

What we desire is that our civil rights shall be guaranteed by law as they are guaranteed to every other class of persons.

Sir, the gentleman from North Carolina who spoke on the questions stated some objections, to which I desire to address a few words of reply. He said it would enforce social rights, and therefore would be detrimental to the interests of both the whites and the blacks of the country. My conception of the effect of this bill, if it be passed into a law, will be simply to place the colored men of this country upon the same footing with every other citizen under the law, and will not at all enforce social relationship with any other class of persons in the country whatsoever. It is merely a matter of law. What we desire is that our civil rights shall be guaranteed by law as they are guaranteed to every other class of persons; and when that is done all other things will come in as a necessary sequence, the enforcement of the rights following the enactment of the law.

Sir, social equality is a right which every man, every woman, and every class of persons have within their own control. They have a right to form their own acquaintances, to establish their own social relationships. Its establishment and regulation is not within the province of legislation. No laws enacted by legislators can compel social equality. Now, what is it we desire? What we desire is this: inasmuch as we have been raised to the dignity, to the honor, to the position of our manhood, we ask that the laws of this country should guarantee all the rights and immunities belonging to that proud position, to be enforced all over this broad land.

Discrimination Exists

Sir, the gentleman states that in the State of North Carolina the colored people enjoy all their rights as far as the highways are concerned; that in the hotels, and in the railroad cars, and in the various public places of resort, they have all the rights and all the immunities accorded to any other class of citizens of the United States. Now, it may not have come under his observation, but it has under mine, that such really is not the case; and the reason why I know and feel it more than he does is because my face is painted black and his is painted white. We who have the color—I may say the objectionable color—know and feel all this. A few days ago, in passing from South Carolina to this city, I entered a place of public resort where hungry men are fed, but I did not dare—I could not without trouble—sit down to the table. I could not sit down at Wilmington or at Weldon without entering into a contest, which I did not desire to do. My colleague, the gentleman who so eloquently spoke on this subject the other day [South Carolina representative Robert Browne Elliott], a few months ago entered a restaurant at Wilmington and sat down to be served, and while there a gentleman stepped up to him and said, "You can not eat here." All the other gentlemen upon the railroad as passengers were eating there; he had only twenty minutes, and was compelled to leave the restaurant or have a fight for it. He showed fight, however, and got his dinner; but he has never been back there since. Coming here last week I felt we did not desire to draw revolvers and present the bold front of warriors, and therefore we ordered our dinners to be brought into the cars, but even there we found the existence of this feeling; for, although we had paid a dollar apiece for our meals, to be brought by the servants into the cars, still there was objection on the part of the railroad people to our eating our meals in the cars, because they said we were putting on airs. They refused us in the restaurant, and then did not desire that we should eat our meals in the cars, although we paid for them. Yet this was in the noble State of North Carolina.

Mr. Speaker, the colored men of the South do not want the adoption of any force measure. No; they do not want anything by force. All they ask is that you will give them, by statutory enactment under the fundamental law, the right to enjoy precisely the same privileges accorded to every other class of citizens.

The gentleman, moreover, has told us that if we pass this civil-rights bill we will thereby rob the colored men of the South of the friendship of the whites. Now, I am at a loss to see how the friendship of our white friends can be lost to us by simply saying we should be permitted to enjoy the rights enjoyed by other citizens. I have a higher opinion of the friendship of the southern men than to suppose any such thing. I know them too well. I know their friendship will not be lost by the passage of this bill. For eight years I have been in South Carolina, and I have found this to be the fact, that the higher class, comprising gentlemen of learning and refinement, are less opposed to this measure than are those who do not occupy so high a position in the social scale.

We have been identified with the interests of this country from its very foundation.

Sir, I think that there will be no difficulty. But I do think this, that there will be more trouble if we do not have those rights. I regard it important, therefore, that we should make the law so strong that no man can infringe those rights.

But, says the gentleman from North Carolina, some ambitious colored man will, when this law is passed, enter a hotel or railroad car, and thus create disturbance. If it be his right, then there is no vaulting ambition in his enjoying that right. And if he can pay for his seat in a first-class car or his room in a hotel, I see no objection to his enjoying it. But the gentleman says more. He cited, on the school question, the evidence of South Carolina, and says the South Carolina University has been destroyed by virtue of bringing into contact the white students with the colored. I think not. It is true that a small number of students left the institution, but the institution still remains. The buildings are there as erect as ever; the faculty are there as attentive to their duties as ever they were; the students are coming in as they did before. It is true, sir, that there is a mixture of students now;

that there are colored and white students of law and medicine sitting side by side; it is true, sir, that the prejudice of some of the professors was so strong that it drove them out of the institution; but the philanthropy and good sense of others were such that they remained; and thus we have still the institution going on, and because some students have left, it cannot be reasonably argued that the usefulness of the institution has been destroyed. The University of South Carolina has not been destroyed.

The Old Ghost of Prejudice

But the gentleman says more. The colored man cannot stand, he says, where this antagonism exists, and he deprecates the idea of antagonizing the races. The gentleman says there is no antagonism on his part. I think there is not antagonism so far as the country is concerned. So far as my observation extends, it goes to prove this: that there is a general acceptance upon the part of the larger and better class of the whites of the South of the situation, and that they regard the education and the development of the colored people as essential to their welfare, and the peace, happiness, and prosperity of the whole country. Many of them, including the best minds of the South, are earnestly engaged in seeking to make this great system of education permanent in all the States. I do not believe, therefore, that it is possible there can be such an antagonism. Why, sir, in Massachusetts there is no such antagonism. There the colored and the white children go to school side by side. In Rhode Island there is not that antagonism. There they are educated side by side in the high schools. In New York, in the highest schools, are to be found of late colored men and colored women. Even old democratic New York does not refuse to give the colored people their rights, and there is no antagonism. A few days ago, when in New York, I made it my business to find out what was the position of matters there in this respect. I ascertained that there are, I think, seven colored ladies in the highest school in New York, and I believe they stand No. 1 in their class, side by side with members of the best and most refined families of the citizens of New York, and without any objection to their presence.

I cannot understand how it is that our southern friends, or a certain class of them, always bring back this old ghost of prejudice and of antagonism. There was a time, not very far distant in the past, when this antagonism was not recognized, when a feeling of fraternization between the white and the colored races existed, that made them kindred to each other. But since our emancipation, since liberty has come, and only since—only since we have stood up clothed in our manhood, only since we have proceeded to take hold and help advance the civilization of this nation—it is only since then that this bugbear is brought up against us again. Sir, the progress of the age demands that the colored man of this country shall be lifted by law into the enjoyment of every right, and that every appliance which is accorded to the German, to the Irishman, to the Englishman, and every foreigner, shall be given to him; and I shall give some reasons why I demand this in the name of justice.

We believe in the Declaration of Independence, that all men are born free and equal.

For two hundred years the colored men of this nation have assisted in building up its commercial interests. There are in this country nearly five millions of us, and for a space of two hundred and forty-seven years we have been hewers of wood and drawers of water; but we have been with you in promoting all the interests of the country. . . .

I propose to state just this: that we have been identified with the interests of this country from its very foundation. The cotton crop of this country has been raised and its rice-fields have been tilled by the hands of our race. All along as the march of progress, as the march of commerce, as the development of your resources has been widening and expanding and spreading, as your vessels have gone on every sea, with the stars and stripes waving over them, and carried your commerce everywhere, there the black man's labor has gone to enrich your country and to augment the grandeur of your nationality. This was done in the time of slavery. And if, for the space of time I have noted, we have been hewers of wood and drawers of water; if we have made your cotton-fields blossom as the rose; if we have made your rice-fields wave with luxuriant harvests; if we have made your corn-fields rejoice; if we have sweated and toiled to build up the prosperity of the whole country by the productions of our labor, I submit, now that the war has made a change, now that we are free—I submit to the nation whether it is not fair and right that we should come in and enjoy to the fullest extent our freedom and liberty.

The Question of Education

A word now as to the question of education. Sir, I know that, indeed, some of our Republican friends are even a little weak on the school clause of this bill [requiring school integration]; but, sir, the education of the race, the education of the nation, is paramount to all other considerations. I regard it important, therefore, that the colored people should take place in the educational march of this nation, and I would suggest that there should be no discrimination. It is against discrimination in this particular that we complain.

Sir, if you look over the reports of superintendents of schools in the several States, you will find, I think, evidences sufficient to warrant Congress in passing the civil-rights bill as it now stands. The report of the commissioner of education of California shows that, under the operation of law and of prejudice, the colored children of that State are practically excluded from schooling. Here is a case where a large class of children are growing up in our midst in a state of ignorance and semi-barbarism. Take the report of the superintendent of education of Indiana, and you will find that while efforts have been made in some places to educate the colored children, yet the prejudice is so great that it debars the colored children from enjoying all the rights which they ought to enjoy under the law. In Illinois, too, the superintendent of education makes this statement: that, while the law guarantees education to every child, yet such are the operations among the school trustees that they almost ignore, in some places, the education of colored children.

All we ask is that you, the legislators of the nation, shall pass a law so strong and so powerful that no one shall be able to elude it and destroy our rights under the Constitution and laws of our country. That is all we ask. . . .

We believe in the Declaration of Independence, that all men are born free and equal, and are endowed by their Creator with certain inalienable rights, among which are life, liberty, and the pursuit of happiness. And we further believe that to secure those rights governments are instituted. And we further believe that when governments cease to subserve those ends the people should change them. . . .

I think it is proper and just that the civil-rights bill should be passed. Some think it would be better to modify it, to strike out the school clause, or to so modify it that some of the State constitutions should not be infringed. I regard it essential to us and the people of this country that we should be secured in this if in nothing else. I cannot regard that our rights will be secured until the jury-box and the school-room, those great palladiums of our liberty, shall have been opened to us. Then we will be willing to take our chances with other men.

I do not ask any legislation for the colored people of this country that is not applied to the white people.

We do not want any discriminations to be made. If discriminations are made in regard to schools, then there will be accomplished just what we are fighting against. If you say that the schools in the State of Georgia, for instance, shall be allowed to discriminate against colored people, then you will have discriminations made against us. We do not want any discriminations. I do not ask any legislation for the colored people of this country that is not applied to the white people. All that we ask is equal laws, equal legislation, and equal rights throughout the length and breadth of this land.

We Are Not Begging

The gentleman from North Carolina also says that the colored men should not come here begging at the doors of Congress for their rights. I agree with him. I want to say that we do not come here begging for our rights. We come here clothed in the garb of American citizenship. We come demanding our rights in the name of justice. We come, with no arrogance on our part, asking, that this great nation, which laid the foundations of civilization and progress more deeply and more securely than any other nation on the face of the earth, guarantee us protection from outrage. We come here, five millions of people—more than composed this whole nation when it had its great tea-party in Boston Harbor, and demanded its rights at the point of the bayonet—asking that unjust discriminations against us be forbidden. We come here in the name of justice, equity, and law, in the name of our children, in the name of our country, petitioning for our rights.

Our rights will yet be accorded to us, I believe, from the feeling that has been exhibited on this floor of the growing sentiment of the country. Rapid as the weaver's shuttle, swift as the lightning's flash, such progress is being made that our rights will be accorded to us ere long. I believe the nation is perfectly willing to accord this measure of justice, if only those who represent the people here would say the word. Let it be proclaimed that henceforth all the children of this land shall be free; that the stars and stripes, waving over all, shall secure to every one equal rights, and the nation will say "amen."

Let the civil-rights bill be passed this day, and five million black men, women, and children, all over the land, will begin a new song of rejoicing, and the thirty-five millions of noble-hearted Anglo-Saxons will join in the shout of joy. Thus will the great mission be fulfilled of giving to all the people equal rights.

Inasmuch as we have toiled with you in building up this nation; inasmuch as we have suffered side by side with you in the war; inasmuch as we have together passed through affliction and pestilence, let there be now a fulfillment of the sublime thought of our fathers—let all men enjoy equal liberty and equal rights. . . .

Our wives and our children have high hopes and aspirations; their longings for manhood and womanhood are equal to those of any other race. The same sentiment of patriotism and of gratitude, the same spirit of national pride that animates the hearts of other citizens animates theirs. In the name of the dead soldiers of our race, whose bodies lie at Petersburgh and on other battle-fields of the South; in the name of the widows and orphans they have left behind; in the name of the widows of the confederate soldiers who fell upon the same fields, I conjure you let this righteous act be done. I appeal to you in the name of God and humanity to give us our rights, for we ask nothing more.

Chapter

Evolving Historical Assessments of Reconstruction

1

Reconstruction Was a Disgraceful Failure

James Ford Rhodes

Well into the twentieth century, the standard interpretation of Reconstruction that students were taught was that it was a shameful period in American history. A typical expression of this view is found in the following excerpt from *History of the United States*, an influential multivolume political history by James Ford Rhodes. Rhodes, a successful Northern industrialist who retired in 1884 at the age of thirty-six to become a historian, contends that Reconstruction failed because it attempted to elevate "inferior" African Americans to a position of political supremacy over whites. Such a policy, in his opinion, proved to be a disaster for both whites and blacks in the South and for the nation as a whole.

No large policy in our country has ever been so conspicuous a failure as that of forcing universal negro suffrage upon the South. The negroes who simply acted out their nature were not to blame. How indeed could they have acquired political honesty? What idea could barbarism thrust into slavery obtain of the rights of property? Even among the Aryans of education and intelligence public integrity has been a plant of slow growth. From the days of the Grecian and Roman republics to our own, men have stolen from the State who would defraud no individual. With his crude ideas of honesty between man and man, what could have been expected of the negro when he got his hand in the public till? The scheme of Reconstruction pan-

James Ford Rhodes, *History of the United States*, Vol. VII (New York: Macmillan, 1918).

dered to the ignorant negroes, the knavish white natives and the vulturous adventurers who flocked from the North; and these neutralized the work of honest Republicans who were officers of State. Intelligence and property stood bound and helpless under negro-carpet-bag rule. And the fact that such governments continued to exist, were supported by Federal authority and defended by prominent Republicans had a share in the demoralization of politics at the North. Senator [Oliver P.] Morton represented the radical view when he declared, "I have no faith in that virtue which assails with fury, fraud and corruption but connives at murder, outrage and oppression." More moderate Republicans, aghast at the corruption prevailing in the Southern governments, lulled an uneasy conscience with the assurance that the Southern

This 1875 drawing from Harper's Weekly *illustrates the belief, popular into the twentieth century, that blacks were politically inferior to whites.*

people had brought the trouble upon themselves. . . . "The whole condition of things at the South is shameful," [New England author James Russell Lowell] wrote, "and I am ready for a movement now to emancipate the whites. No doubt the government is bound to protect the misintelligence of the blacks, but surely not at the expense of the intelligence of men of our own blood. The South on the whole has behaved better than I expected but our extremists expect them to like being told once a week that they have been *licked.*"

No large policy in our country has ever been so conspicuous a failure as that of forcing universal negro suffrage upon the South.

From the Republican policy came no real good to the negroes. Most of them developed no political capacity, and the few who raised themselves above the mass did not reach a high order of intelligence. At different periods two served in the United States Senate, twenty in the House; they left no mark on the legislation of their time; none of them, in comparison with their white associates, attained the least distinction. When the Southern States recovered home rule, negroes were of course no longer sent to Congress from the South but they have had a fair chance at the North where they obtained the suffrage in every State within a few years after the Civil War. Politically very active and numerous enough in some of the Northern States to form a political force, that has to be reckoned with, no one of them (I believe) has ever been sent to Congress; few get into legislature or city council. Very few if any are elected to administrative offices of responsibility. The negro's political activity is rarely of a nature to identify him with any movement on a high plane. . . . In a word he has been politically a failure and he could not have been otherwise. In spite of all the warnings of science and political experience, he was started at the top and, as is the fate of most such unfortunates, he fell to the bottom.

The Negro's Fate

Truly the negro's fate has been hard. Torn from his native land he was made a slave to satisfy the white man's greed.

At last, owing to a great moral movement, he gained the long-wished-for boon of freedom; and then when in intellect still a child, instead of being treated as a child, taught gradually the use of his liberty and given rights in the order of his development, he, without any demand of his own, was raised at once to the white man's political estate, partly for the partisan designs of those who had freed him. His old masters, who understood him best and who, chastened by defeat and by adversity, were really his best friends, were alienated. He fell into the hands of rascals who through his vote fattened on the spoils of office. He had a brief period of mastery and indulgence during which his mental and moral education was deplorable and his worst passions were catered to. Finally by force, by craft and by law his old masters have deprived him of the ballot and, after a number of years of political power, he has been set back to the point, where he should have started directly after emancipation. He is trying to learn the lesson of life with the work made doubly hard by the Saturnalia [unrestrained celebration] he has passed through.

Republican Party Failures

The Congressional policy of Reconstruction was short-sighted even from the partisan point of view in that it gave the South a grievance. In that balancing of rights and wrongs, which must be made in a just consideration of a great human transaction, the North at the end of the war could appeal to Europe and to history for the justification of its belief that there was on its side a large credit balance. Some of this it has lost by its repressive, uncivilized and unsuccessful policy of Reconstruction. Moreover the close sequence of events has led the South to regard negro rule as the complement of emancipation with the result that she has sometimes lost sight of the benefit of the great act which gave freedom to the slaves.

The Congressional policy of Reconstruction was short-sighted.

An avowed aim of the Congressional policy of Reconstruction was to build up a Republican party at the South. Here was a failure complete and an opportunity missed.

The nucleus of a Republican party was there in the old-line whigs and Union-men-who-went-with-their-State. . . . At the end of the war they were ready to act in opposition to the secession Democrats and fire-eaters . . . but the policy of Congress, which raised the race issue, consolidated all the white men into one party for self-protection. Some Southern men at first acted with the Republican party but they gradually slipped away from it as the colour line was drawn and reckless and corrupt financial legislation inaugurated. No doubt can exist that, if negro suffrage had not been forced upon the South, a healthy and respectable Republican party would have been formed, attaining perhaps the power and influence which the Democrats have in New England and in contests like those of 1896 and 1900, furnishing electoral votes for the Republican presidential candidate. And so far as we can divine, had the matter been left to the States themselves, suffrage by this time [1906] would have been fully accorded to the negroes on the basis of educational and property qualifications.

Praising Southern Leaders

What manner of people were they with whom the North had to deal at the close of the war? Let them be described by George F. Hoar, always a stiff Republican partisan on the Southern question. . . . "Although my life politically and personally," he wrote, "has been a life of almost constant strife with the leaders of the Southern people, yet, as I grow older, I have learned, not only to respect and esteem, but to love the great qualities which belong to my fellow-citizens of the Southern States. They are a noble race. We may well take pattern from them in some of the great virtues which make up the strength, as they make the glory of Free States. Their love of home; their chivalrous respect for woman; their courage; their delicate sense of honor; their constancy which can abide by an opinion or a purpose or an interest of their States through adversity and through prosperity, through the years and through the generations, are things by which the people of the more mercurial North may take a lesson. And there is another thing—covetousness, corruption, the low temptation of money has not yet found any place in our Southern politics."

These were the men we delivered over into the hands of the negroes and their partisan or corrupt leaders. But adversity did not crush them. President F.A.P. Barnard of Columbia College, a man who knew both the South and the North, wrote on February 16, 1878, "It is indeed a marvellous thing how, after her trials, the South still continues to maintain her noble pre-eminence in statesmanship and in moral dignity."

2

Reconstruction Was Not a Disgraceful Failure

W.E.B. Du Bois

It is perhaps not surprising that some of the earliest challenges to traditional Reconstruction historiography and its assumptions about black inferiority came from black scholars and historians, including Carter G. Woodson, John Hope Franklin, and W.E.B. Du Bois. In 1909 Du Bois, the first African American to earn a Ph.D. from Harvard University, presented a paper before the American Historical Association in which he defended Reconstruction-era reforms. He argues that Reconstruction was a time of great improvement in the education and economic and political status of the newly freed slaves in the South. Du Bois also defends the state governments (which African Americans voted for and participated in) against charges of corruption and failure. Du Bois's views on Reconstruction became widely accepted among revisionist historians in the 1950s and 1960s.

Du Bois had a long and distinguished career as a historian, sociologist, and civil rights activist. His books include *Black Reconstruction*, published in 1935.

There is danger to-day [1909] that between the intense feeling of the South and the conciliatory spirit of the North grave injustice will be done the Negro American in the history of Reconstruction. Those who see in Negro suffrage the cause of the main evils of Reconstruction must remember that if there had not been a single freedman left in the South after the war the problems of Reconstruction

W.E.B. Du Bois, "Reconstruction and Its Benefits," *American Historical Review*, Vol. 15, July 1910, pp. 781–99.

would still have been grave. Property in slaves to the extent of perhaps two thousand million dollars had suddenly disappeared. One thousand five hundred more millions, representing the Confederate war debt, had largely disappeared. Large amounts of real estate and other property had been destroyed, industry had been disorganized, 250,000 men had been killed and many more maimed. With this went the moral effect of an unsuccessful war with all its letting down of social standards and quickening of hatred and discouragement—a situation which would make it difficult under any circumstances to reconstruct a new government and a new civilization. Add to all this the presence of four million freedmen and the situation is further complicated. . . .

Seldom in the history of the world has an almost totally illiterate population been given the means of self-education in so short a time.

How to train and treat these ex-slaves easily became a central problem of Reconstruction, although by no means the only problem. Three agencies undertook the solution of this problem at first and their influence is apt to be forgotten. Without them the problems of Reconstruction would have been far graver than they were. These agencies were: (a) the Negro church, (b) the Negro school, and (c) the Freedmen's Bureau. After the war the white churches of the South got rid of their Negro members and the Negro church organizations of the North invaded the South. The 20,000 members of the African Methodist Episcopal Church in 1856 leaped to 75,000 in 1866 and 200,000 in 1876, while their property increased sevenfold. The Negro Baptists with 150,000 members in 1850 had fully a half million in 1870. There were, before the end of Reconstruction, perhaps 10,000 local bodies touching the majority of the freed population, centering almost the whole of their social life, and teaching them organization and autonomy. They were primitive, ill-governed, at times fantastic groups of human beings, and yet it is difficult to exaggerate the influence of this new responsibility—the first social institution fully controlled by black men in America, with traditions that rooted back to Africa and with possibilities which make the 35,000 Negro American churches to-day, with their three and one-half million members, the most powerful Negro institutions in the world.

With the Negro church, but separate from it, arose the school as the first expression of the missionary activity of Northern religious bodies. Seldom in the history of the world has an almost totally illiterate population been given the means of self-education in so short a time. The movement started with the Negroes themselves and they continued to form the dynamic force behind it. . . . The education of this mass had to begin at the top with the training of teachers, and within a few years a dozen colleges and normal schools started; by 1877, 571,506 Negro children were in school. There can be no doubt that these schools were a great conservative steadying force to which the South owes much. It must not be forgotten that among the agents of the Freedmen's Bureau were not only soldiers and politicians but school-teachers and educational leaders like Edmund Ware and Erastus Cravath.

Questions Facing Politicians

Granted that the situation was in any case bad and that Negro churches and schools stood as conservative educative forces, how far did Negro suffrage hinder progress, and was it expedient? The difficulties that stared Reconstruction politicians in the face were these: (a) They must act quickly. (b) Emancipation had increased the political power of the South by one-sixth: could this increased political power be put in the hands of those who, in defense of slavery, had disrupted the Union? (c) How was the abolition of slavery to be made effective? (d) What was to be the political position of the freedmen?

Andrew Johnson said in 1864, in regard to calling a convention to restore the state of Tennessee,

> who shall restore and re-establish it? Shall the man who gave his influence and his means to destroy the Government? Is he to participate in the great work of re-organization? Shall he who brought this misery upon the State be permitted to control its destinies? If this be so, then all this precious blood of our brave soldiers and officers so freely poured out will have been wantonly spilled.

To settle these and other difficulties, three ways were

suggested: (1) the Freedmen's Bureau, (2) partial Negro suffrage, and (3) full manhood suffrage for Negroes.

The Freedmen's Bureau was an attempt to establish a government guardianship over the Negroes and insure their economic and civil rights. Its establishment was a herculean task both physically and socially, and it not only met the solid opposition of the white South, but even the North looked at the new thing as socialistic and over-paternal. It accomplished a great task but it was repudiated. Carl Schurz in 1865 felt warranted in saying

> that not half of the labor that has been done in the south this year, or will be done there next year, would have been or would be done but for the exertions of the Freedmen's Bureau. . . . No other agency, except one placed there by the national government, could have wielded that moral power whose interposition was so necessary to prevent the southern society from falling at once into the chaos of a general collision between its different elements.

Notwithstanding this the Bureau was temporary, was regarded as a makeshift and soon abandoned.

The arguments for universal Negro suffrage from the start were strong and are still strong.

Meantime, partial Negro suffrage seemed not only just but almost inevitable. Lincoln in 1864 "cautiously suggested" to Louisiana's private consideration, "whether some of the colored people may not be let in, as, for instance, the very intelligent, and especially those who fought gallantly in our ranks. They would probably help, in some trying to come, to keep the jewel of liberty in the family of freedom." Indeed, the "family of freedom" in Louisiana being somewhat small just then, who else was to be intrusted with the "jewel"? Later and for different reasons, Johnson in 1865 wrote to Mississippi:

> If you could extend the elective franchise to all persons of color who can read the Constitution of the United States in English and write their names, and to all persons of color who own real estate valued at not less

than two hundred and fifty dollars, and pay taxes thereon, you would completely disarm the adversary and set an example the other States will follow. This you can do with perfect safety, and you thus place the southern States, in reference to free persons of color, upon the same basis with the free States. I hope and trust your convention will do this.

Meantime the Negroes themselves began to ask for the suffrage—the Georgia Convention in Augusta, 1866, advocating "a proposition to give those who could write and read well, and possessed a certain property qualification, the right of suffrage." The reply of the South to these suggestions was decisive. In Tennessee alone was any action attempted that even suggested possible Negro suffrage in the future, and that failed. In all other states the "Black Codes" adopted were certainly not reassuring to friends of freedom. To be sure it was not a time to look for calm, cool, thoughtful action on the part of the white South. Their economic condition was pitiable, their fear of Negro freedom genuine; yet it was reasonable to expect from them something less than repression and utter reaction toward slavery. To some extent this expectation was fulfilled: the abolition of slavery was recognized and the civil rights of owning property and appearing as a witness in cases in which he was a party were generally granted the Negro; yet with these went in many cases harsh and unbearable regulations which largely neutralized the concessions and certainly gave ground for the assumption that once free the South would virtually re-enslave the Negro. The colored people themselves naturally feared this and protested as in Mississippi "against the reactionary policy prevailing, and expressing the fear that the Legislature will pass such proscriptive laws as will drive the freedmen from the State, or practically re-enslave them."

The Codes spoke for themselves. They have often been reprinted and quoted. No open-minded student can read them without being convinced that they meant nothing more nor less than slavery in daily toil. . . .

All things considered, it seems probable that if the South had been permitted to have its way in 1865 the harshness of Negro slavery would have been mitigated so as to make slave-trading difficult, and to make it possible for a

Negro to hold property and appear in some cases in court; but that in most other respects the blacks would have remained in slavery.

What could prevent this? A Freedmen's Bureau, established for ten, twenty or forty years with a careful distribution of land and capital and a system of education for the children, might have prevented such an extension of slavery. But the country would not listen to such a comprehensive plan. A restricted grant of the suffrage voluntarily made by the states would have been reassuring proof of a desire to treat the freedmen fairly, and would have balanced, in part at least, the increased political power of the South. There was no such disposition evident. . . .

Three Possible Courses
The United States government might now have taken any one of three courses:
1. Allowed the whites to reorganize the states and take no measures to enfranchise the freedmen.
2. Allowed the whites to reorganize the states but provided that after the lapse of a reasonable length of time there should be no discrimination in the right of suffrage on account of "race, color or previous condition of servitude."
3. Admitted all men, black and white, to take part in reorganizing the states and then provided that future restrictions on the suffrage should be made on any basis except "race, color and previous condition of servitude."

The first course was clearly inadmissible since it meant virtually giving up the great principle on which the war was largely fought and won, *i.e.*, human freedom; a giving of freedom which contented itself with an edict, and then turned the "freed" slaves over to the tender mercies of their impoverished and angry ex-masters was no gift at all. The second course was theoretically attractive but practically impossible. It meant at least a prolongation of slavery and instead of attempts to raise the freedmen, it gave the white community strong incentives for keeping the blacks down so that as few as possible would ever qualify for the suffrage. Negro schools would have been discouraged and economic fetters would have held the black man as a serf for an indefinite time. On the other hand, the arguments for universal

Negro suffrage from the start were strong and are still strong, and no one would question their strength were it not for the assumption that the experiment failed. Frederick Douglass said to President Johnson: "Your noble and humane predecessor placed in our hands the sword to assist in saving the nation, and we do hope that you, his able successor, will favorably regard the placing in our hands the ballot with which to save ourselves." And when Johnson demurred on account of the hostility between blacks and poor whites, a committee of prominent colored men replied:

> Even if it were true, as you allege, that the hostility of the blacks toward the poor whites must necessarily project itself into a state of freedom, and that this enmity between the two races is even more intense in a state of freedom than in a state of slavery, in the name of Heaven, we reverently ask, how can you, in view of your professed desire to promote the welfare of the black man, deprive him of all means of defence, and clothe him whom you regard as his enemy in the panoply of political power? . . .

The steps that ended in the Fifteenth Amendment were not, however, taken suddenly. The Negroes were given the right by universal suffrage to join in reconstructing the state governments and the reasons for it were cogently set forth in the report of the Joint Committee on Reconstruction in 1866, which began as follows:

> A large proportion of the population had become, instead of mere chattels, free men and citizens. Through all the past struggle these had remained true and loyal, and had, in large numbers, fought on the side of the Union. It was impossible to abandon them without securing them their rights as free men and citizens. The whole civilized world would have cried out against such base ingratitude, and the bare idea is offensive to all right-thinking men. Hence it became important to inquire what could be done to secure their rights, civil and political.

The Results of Negro Suffrage

For such reasons the Negro was enfranchised. What was the result? No language has been spared to describe these results as the worst imaginable. Nor is it necessary to dispute for a moment that there were bad results, and bad results arising from Negro suffrage; but it may be questioned if the results were as bad as painted or if Negro suffrage was the prime cause.

Let us not forget that the white South believed it to be of vital interest to its welfare that the experiment of Negro suffrage should fail ignominiously, and that almost to a man the whites were willing to insure this failure either by active force or passive acquiescence; that beside this there were, as might be expected, men, black and white, Northern and Southern, only too eager to take advantage of such a situation for feathering their own nests. The results in such case had to be evil but to charge the evil to Negro suffrage is unfair. It may be charged to anger, poverty, venality, and ignorance; but the anger and poverty were the almost inevitable aftermath of war; the venality was much greater among whites than Negroes, and while ignorance was the curse of the Negroes, the fault was not theirs, and they took the initiative to correct it.

In the midst of . . . difficulties the Negro governments in the South accomplished much of positive good.

The chief charges against the Negro governments are extravagance, theft, and incompetency of officials. There is no serious charge that these governments threatened civilization or the foundations of social order. The charge is that they threatened property, and that they were inefficient. These charges are in part undoubtedly true, but they are often exaggerated. . . .

Undoubtedly there were many ridiculous things connected with Reconstruction governments: the placing of ignorant field-hands who could neither read nor write in the legislature, the gold spittoons of South Carolina, the enormous public printing bill of Mississippi—all these were extravagant and funny, and yet somehow, to one who sees beneath all that is bizarre, the real human tragedy of the upward striving of down-trodden men, the groping for light among people born in darkness, there is less tendency to laugh and gibe than among shallower minds and easier consciences. All that is funny is not bad.

Then too a careful examination of the alleged stealing in the South reveals much. First, there is repeated exaggeration. For instance it is said that the taxation in Mississippi was *fourteen* times as great in 1874 as in 1869. This sounds staggering until we learn that the state taxation in 1869 was only ten cents on one hundred dollars, and that the expenses of government in 1874 were only twice as great as in 1860, and that too with a depreciated currency. It could certainly be argued that the state government in Mississippi was doing enough additional work in 1874 to warrant greatly increased cost. A Southern white historian [James W. Garner] acknowledges that

> the work of restoration which the government was obliged to undertake, made increased expenses necessary. During the period of the war, and for several years thereafter, public buildings and state institutions were permitted to fall into decay. The state house and grounds, the executive mansion, the penitentiary, the insane asylum, and the buildings for the blind, deaf, and dumb were in a dilapidated condition, and had to be extended and repaired. A new building for the blind was purchased and fitted up. The reconstructionists established a public school system and spent money to maintain and support it, perhaps too freely, in view of the impoverishment of the people. When they took hold, warrants were worth but sixty or seventy cents on the dollar, a fact which made the price of building materials used in the work of construction correspondingly higher. So far as the conduct of state officials who were intrusted with the custody of public funds is concerned, it may be said that there were no great embezzlements or other cases of misappropriation during the period of Republican rule.

The state debt of Mississippi was said to have been increased from a half million to twenty million when in fact it had not been increased at all.

The character of the real thieving shows that white men must have been the chief beneficiaries. . . .

The frauds through the manipulation of state and railway bonds and of bank-notes must have inured chiefly to the benefit of experienced white men, and this must have been largely the case in the furnishing and printing frauds. It was chiefly in the extravagance for "sundries and incidentals" and direct money payments for votes that the Negroes received their share.

That the Negroes led by astute thieves became tools and received a small share of the spoils is true. But two considerations must be added: much of the legislation which resulted in fraud was represented to the Negroes as good legislation, and thus their votes were secured by deliberate misrepresentation. . . .

There is no doubt but that the thirst of the black man for knowledge . . . gave birth to the public free-school system of the South.

Granted then that the Negroes were to some extent venal but to a much larger extent ignorant and deceived, the question is: did they show any signs of a disposition to learn better things? The theory of democratic government is not that the will of the people is always right, but rather that normal human beings of average intelligence will, if given a chance, learn the right and best course by bitter experience. This is precisely what the Negro voters showed indubitable signs of doing. First, they strove for schools to abolish ignorance, and, second, a large and growing number of them revolted against the carnival of extravagance and stealing that marred the beginning of Reconstruction, and joined with the best elements to institute reform. . . . The greatest stigma on the white South is not that it opposed Negro suffrage and resented theft and incompetence, but that when it saw the reform movement growing and even in some cases triumphing, and a larger and larger number of black voters learning to vote for honesty and ability, it still preferred a Reign of Terror to a campaign of education, and disfranchised Negroes instead of punishing rascals. . . .

In the midst of all these difficulties the Negro governments in the South accomplished much of positive good. We may recognize three things which Negro rule gave to the South:

1. Democratic government.
2. Free public schools.
3. New social legislation.

Two states will illustrate conditions of government in the South before and after Negro rule. In South Carolina there was before the war a property qualification for office-holders, and, in part, for voters. The Constitution of 1868, on the other hand, was a modern democratic document starting (in marked contrast to the old constitutions) with a declaration that "We, the People," framed it, and preceded by a broad Declaration of Rights which did away with property qualifications and based representation directly upon population instead of property. It especially took up new subjects of social legislation, declaring navigable rivers free public highways, instituting homestead exemptions, establishing boards of county commissioners, providing for a new penal code of laws, establishing universal manhood suffrage "without distinction of race or color," devoting six sections to charitable and penal institutions and six to corporations, providing separate property for married women, etc. Above all, eleven sections of the Tenth Article were devoted to the establishment of a complete public-school system.

So satisfactory was the constitution thus adopted by Negro suffrage and by a convention composed of a majority of blacks that the state lived twenty-seven years under it without essential change and when the constitution was revised in 1895, the revision was practically nothing more than an amplification of the Constitution of 1868. No essential advance step of the former document was changed except the suffrage article.

In Mississippi the Constitution of 1868 was, as compared with that before the war, more democratic. It not only forbade distinctions on account of color but abolished all property qualifications for jury service, and property and educational qualifications for office; it prohibited the lending of the credit of the state for private corporations—an abuse dating back as far as 1830. It increased the powers of the governor, raised the low state salaries, and increased the number of state officials. New ideas like the public-school system and the immigration bureau were introduced and in general the activity of the state greatly and necessarily enlarged. Finally, that was the only constitution ever submitted in popular approval at the polls. This constitution remained in force twenty-two years.

In general the words of Judge Albion W. Tourgee, a "carpetbagger," are true when he says of the Negro governments:

They obeyed the Constitution of the United States, and annulled the bonds of states, counties, and cities which had been issued to carry on the war of rebellion and maintain armies in the field against the Union. They instituted a public school system in a realm where public schools had been unknown. They opened the ballot box and jury box to thousands of white men who had been debarred from them by a lack of earthly possessions. They introduced home rule to the South. They abolished the whipping post, the branding iron, the stocks and other barbarous forms of punishment which had up to that time prevailed. They reduced capital felonies from about twenty to two or three. In an age of extravagance they were extravagant in the sums appropriated for public works. In all of that time no man's rights of person were invaded under the forms of law. Every Democrat's life, home, fireside and business were safe. No man obstructed any white man's way to the ballot box, interfered with his freedom of speech, or boycotted him on account of his political faith.

A thorough study of the legislation accompanying these constitutions and its changes since would of course be necessary before a full picture of the situation could be given. This has not been done, but so far as my studies have gone I have been surprised at the comparatively small amount of change in law and government which the overthrow of Negro rule brought about. . . .

Reconstruction and Education

There is no doubt but that the thirst of the black man for knowledge—a thirst which has been too persistent and durable to be mere curiosity or whim—gave birth to the public free-school system of the South. It was the question upon which black voters and legislators insisted more than anything else and while it is possible to find some vestiges of free schools in some of the Southern States before the war yet a universal, well-established system dates from the day that the black man got political power. . . .

We are apt to forget that in all human probability the granting of Negro manhood suffrage and the passage of the Fifteenth Amendment were decisive in rendering permanent the foundation of the Negro common school. Even after the overthrow of the Negro governments, if the Negroes had been left a servile caste, personally free, but politically powerless, it is not reasonable to think that a system of common schools would have been provided for them by the Southern States. Serfdom and education have ever proven contradictory terms. But when Congress, backed by the nation, determined to make the Negroes full-fledged voting citizens, the South had a hard dilemma before her: either to keep the Negroes under as an ignorant proletariat and stand the chance of being ruled eventually from the slums and jails, or to join in helping to raise these wards of the nation to a position of intelligence and thrift by means of a public-school system. . . .

Finally, in legislation covering property, the wider functions of the state, the punishment of crime and the like, it is sufficient to say that the laws on these points established by Reconstruction legislatures were not only different from and even revolutionary to the laws in the older South, but they were so wise and so well suited to the needs of the new South that in spite of a retrogressive movement following the overthrow of the Negro governments the mass of this legislation, with elaboration and development, still stands on the statue books of the South. . . .

Paint the "carpet-bag" governments and Negro rule as black as may be, the fact remains that the essence of the revolution which the overturning of the Negro governments made was to put these black men and their friends out of power. Outside the curtailing of expenses and stopping of extravagance, not only did their successors make few changes in the work which these legislatures and conventions had done, but they largely carried out their plans, followed their suggestions, and strengthened their institutions. Practically the whole new growth of the South has been accomplished under laws which black men helped to frame thirty years ago. I know of no greater compliment to Negro suffrage.

Chronology

January 1, 1863
President Abraham Lincoln signs the Emancipation Proclamation.

December 8, 1863
Lincoln announces his Proclamation of Amnesty, which delineates his Ten Percent Plan for Reconstruction.

July 2, 1864
Congress passes the Wade-Davis Bill, which is designed to give Congress control over Reconstruction. Lincoln pocket-vetoes the bill two days later.

November 8, 1864
President Lincoln is elected to a second term.

January 16, 1865
General William T. Sherman issues Special Field Order Number 15, which sets aside portions of Southern land for the exclusive settlement of the freed slaves.

January 31, 1865
Congress approves the Thirteenth Amendment by a vote of 119–56.

March 3, 1865
The Bureau for Refugees, Freedmen, and Abandoned Lands, known as the Freedmen's Bureau, is established by an act of Congress.

April 9, 1865
Confederate general Robert E. Lee surrenders to Union general Ulysses S. Grant at Appomattox Courthouse.

April 11, 1865
President Lincoln delivers his last public address, in which he endorses limited black suffrage.

April 14, 1865
Lincoln is shot by John Wilkes Booth; he dies the next day. Three hours after Lincoln's death, Vice President Andrew Johnson takes the presidential oath of office.

May 29, 1865
President Johnson announces his Reconstruction policy, which grants pardons to former Rebels who pledge loyalty to the Union.

July 1865
General Oliver Howard, commissioner of the Freedmen's Bureau, issues Circular 13 instructing bureau agents to set aside forty-acre tracts of land for the freedmen.

September 1865
Johnson instructs Howard to rescind Circular 13. In October, Howard announces to black settlers that their land will be returned to the original white owners.

November 24, 1865
Mississippi becomes the first state to enact a Black Code. Most of the other Southern states shortly follow suit.

December 18, 1865
The Thirteenth Amendment is ratified.

April 9, 1866
Overriding a presidential veto, Congress passes the Civil Rights Act of 1866.

May 1–3, 1866
A major race riot erupts in Memphis, Tennessee; forty-six blacks and two white Unionists are killed.

June 13, 1866
Congress approves the Fourteenth Amendment.

July 24, 1866
Congress readmits Tennessee to the Union.

July 30, 1866
A race riot breaks out in New Orleans. Thirty-four blacks and three white Radicals are among the forty casualties.

November 1866
Republicans sweep the congressional elections, providing them with the majority needed to consistently override presidential vetoes.

March 2, 1867
Congress enacts two bills over Johnson's veto: the First Reconstruction Act, which divides the former Confederacy into five military districts, and the Tenure of Office Act, which prohibits the president from dismissing a cabinet officer without the Senate's consent.

March 23, 1867
The Second Reconstruction Act is passed by Congress over a presidential veto.

July 19, 1867
Congress passes the Third Reconstruction Act over a presidential veto.

August 12, 1867
President Johnson suspends War Secretary Edwin Stanton and asks the Senate to agree to his dismissal under the terms of the Tenure of Office Act.

November 5, 1867
In Montgomery, Alabama, the first Reconstruction state constitutional convention begins. During the following months, all of the former Confederate states hold conventions.

January 13, 1868
The Senate declines to remove Stanton from his cabinet office.

February 21, 1868
Johnson dismisses Stanton, who refuses to leave and barricades himself in his office.

February 24, 1868
The House of Representatives votes 126–47 to impeach President Johnson.

March 11, 1868
Congress passes the Fourth Reconstruction Act.

March 13, 1868
Johnson's impeachment trial begins.

May 28, 1868
The Senate acquits President Johnson of high crimes and misdemeanors.

June 22–25, 1868
Congress readmits Alabama, Arkansas, North Carolina, South Carolina, Louisiana, Florida, and Georgia to the Union.

July 21, 1868
The Fourteenth Amendment is ratified.

September 1868
After Georgia's state government removes its black members, Congress returns Georgia to military rule.

November 3, 1868
General Ulysses S. Grant is elected president.

February 26, 1869
Congress approves the Fifteenth Amendment.

January 20, 1870
Hiram R. Revels of Mississippi is elected as the first black U.S. senator.

January 26, 1870
Congress readmits Virginia to the Union.

February 23, 1870
Mississippi is readmitted to the Union.

March 30, 1870
The Fifteenth Amendment is ratified. In the following months, several Southern states pass poll-tax laws that are designed to reduce the effectiveness of the Fifteenth Amendment by restricting black voters. Texas is readmitted to the Union.

May 31, 1870
Congress passes the First Enforcement Act in an effort to deal with increasing violence and civil rights violations in the South.

July 15, 1870
Congress readmits Georgia to the Union for the second time.

October 25, 1870
In Eutaw, Alabama, whites fire into a Republican campaign rally, killing four blacks and wounding fifty.

February 28, 1871
Congress passes the Second Enforcement Act.

March 4, 1871
The first black representatives to the U.S. Congress take their seats. They are Joseph H. Rainey, Robert DeLarge, Robert Brown Elliot, Benjamin S. Turner, and Josiah T. Walls.

March 6–7, 1871
In Meridian, Mississippi, a white Republican judge and more than thirty blacks are killed during a race riot.

April 20, 1871
Congress passes the Third Enforcement Act, also called the Ku Klux Klan Act.

October 17, 1871
President Grant sends federal troops to South Carolina to put down the Ku Klux Klan.

May 22, 1872
Congress passes the Amnesty Act, which removes political disabilities from all but approximately five hundred of the most prominent former Confederates.

June 10, 1872
The Freedmen's Bureau Act is allowed to expire, and the bureau is dissolved.

November 5, 1872
In a landslide victory, President Grant is elected to a second term.

December 9, 1872
P.B.S. Pinchback of Louisiana becomes the first black governor in America when Louisiana's sitting governor is suspended due to impeachment proceedings.

April 13, 1873
On Easter Sunday, more than sixty blacks are killed by armed whites in Colfax, Louisiana.

April 14, 1873
In the Slaughterhouse Cases, the U.S. Supreme Court rules that the Fourteenth Amendment protects only those rights that derive from federal—not state—citizenship.

September 18, 1873
The failure of a major banking firm triggers the Panic of 1873, an economic depression that persists for five years.

November 4, 1874
Democrats sweep the congressional elections and gain a majority in the House of Representatives.

December 7, 1874
On December 7 and the following days, bands of armed whites kill an estimated three hundred blacks in Vicksburg, Mississippi.

January 5, 1875
President Grant dispatches federal troops to Vicksburg, Mississippi.

February 3, 1875
Blanche K. Bruce is elected to the U.S. Senate, bringing black representation in Congress to its Reconstruction-era peak of eight.

March 1, 1875
Congress passes the Civil Rights Act of 1875, which outlaws segregation.

March 1875
Congress fails to pass a Fourth Enforcement Bill before adjourning.

September 4–6, 1875
Thirty blacks and three whites are killed in a race riot in Clinton, Mississippi.

March 27, 1876
In *U.S. v. Cruikshank*, the U.S. Supreme Court overturns convictions under the Enforcement Act of 1870, ruling that the federal government can only prohibit civil rights violations by the states, not by private individuals.

July 8, 1876
A race riot in Hamburg, South Carolina, results in the deaths of seven blacks.

September 20, 1876
A race riot erupts in Ellenton, South Carolina; several whites and approximately one hundred blacks are killed.

October 16, 1876
Six whites and one black die in a race riot in Cainhoy, South Carolina.

October 26, 1876
Grant sends federal troops to intervene in South Carolina.

November 7, 1876
The presidential election results in a dispute over who won.

February 26, 1877
The Compromise of 1877 secures Republican Rutherford B. Hayes's claim to the presidency in exchange for the return of home rule to the South.

April 24, 1877
Hayes withdraws the last federal troops from the South.

For Further Research

Books

Herman Belz, *Emancipation and Equal Rights*. New York: Norton, 1978.

Michael Les Benedict, *The Impeachment and Trial of Andrew Johnson*. New York: Norton, 1973.

Lerone Bennett, *Black Power, U.S.A.: The Human Side of Reconstruction, 1867–1877*. Chicago: Johnson, 1967.

Dan Carter, *When the War Was Over: The Failure of Self-Reconstruction in the South, 1865–1867*. Baton Rouge: Louisiana State University Press, 1985.

Richard N. Current, *Those Terrible Carpetbaggers*. New York: Oxford University Press, 1988.

W.E.B. Du Bois, *Black Reconstruction in America: 1860–1880*. New York: Russell & Russell, 1935.

William Dunning, *Reconstruction: Political and Economic, 1865–1877*. New York: Harper, 1907.

Eric Foner, *A Short History of Reconstruction, 1863–1877*. New York: Harper & Row, 1990.

Eric Foner and Olivia Mahoney, *America's Reconstruction: People and Politics After the Civil War*. Baton Rouge: Louisiana State University Press, 1997.

Harold M. Hyman, ed., *New Frontiers of the American Reconstitution*. Urbana: University of Illinois Press, 1966.

Stetson Kennedy, *After Appomattox: How the South Won the War*. Gainesville: University Press of Florida, 1995.

Leon Litwack, *Been in the Storm So Long: The Aftermath of Slavery*. New York: Knopf, 1979.

James M. McPherson, *Ordeal by Fire: The Civil War and Reconstruction*. New York: Knopf, 1982.

Donald G. Nieman, *To Set the Law in Motion: The Freedmen's Bureau and the Legal Rights of Blacks*. Millwood, NY: KTO Press, 1979.

Michael Perman, *Emancipation and Reconstruction: 1862–1879*. Arlington Heights, IL: Harlan Davidson, 1987.

George Rable, *But There Was No Peace: The Role of Violence in the Politics of Reconstruction*. Athens: University of Georgia Press, 1984.

James L. Roark, *Masters Without Slaves: Southern Planters in the Civil War and Reconstruction*. New York: Norton, 1977.

Nina Silber, *The Romance of Reunion: Northerners and the South, 1865–1900*. Chapel Hill: University of North Carolina Press, 1993.

Kenneth Stampp, *The Era of Reconstruction, 1865–1877*. New York: Knopf, 1965.

Hans L. Trefousse, *Impeachment of a President: Andrew Johnson, the Blacks, and Reconstruction*. Knoxville: University of Tennessee Press, 1975.

Allen W. Trelease, *White Terror: The Ku Klux Klan Conspiracy and Southern Reconstruction*. New York: Harper & Row, 1971.

C. Vann Woodward, *Reunion and Reaction: The Compromise of 1877 and the End of Reconstruction*. New York: Oxford University Press, 1991.

Primary Sources and Document Collections

LaWanda Cox and John H. Cox, eds., *Reconstruction, the Negro, and the New South*. Columbia: University of South Carolina Press, 1973.

Richard N. Current, ed., *Reconstruction, 1865–1877*. Englewood Cliffs, NJ: Prentice-Hall, 1965.

Harold M. Hyman, ed., *The Radical Republicans and Reconstruction, 1861–1870*. Indianapolis: Bobbs-Merrill, 1967.

Annjennette Sophie McFarlin, ed., *Black Congressional Reconstruction Orators and Their Orations, 1869–1879*. Metuchen, NJ: Scarecrow Press, 1976.

James S. Pike, *The Prostrate State: South Carolina Under Negro Government*. New York: D. Appleton, 1874.

Dorothy Sterling, ed., *The Trouble They Seen: Black People Tell the Story of Reconstruction*. Garden City, NY: Doubleday, 1976.

Brenda Stevenson, ed., *The Journals of Charlotte Forten Grimke*. New York: Oxford University Press, 1988.

Harvey Wish, ed., *Reconstruction in the South, 1865–1877.* New York: Farrar, Straus, 1964.

Periodicals

Craig E. Blohm, "Reconstructing America," *Cobblestone,* February 2001.

Eric Foner, "The New View of Reconstruction," *American Heritage,* October 1983.

John Hope Franklin, "Mirror for Americans: A Century of Reconstruction History," *American Historical Review,* February 1980.

John Harrison, "The Lawfulness of the Reconstruction Amendments," *University of Chicago Law Review,* Spring 2001.

William S. McFeely, "Two Reconstructions, Two Nations," *Massachusetts Review,* Spring 1991.

Paul Moreno, "Racial Classifications and Reconstruction Legislation," *Journal of Southern History,* May 1995.

Clyde Wilson, "War, Reconstruction, and the End of the Old Republic," *Society,* September/October 1996.

Richard Zuczek, "The Last Campaign of the Civil War: South Carolina and the Revolution of 1876," *Civil War History,* March 1996.

Websites

Jensen's Guide to Reconstruction History, 1861–1877, http://tigger.uic.edu
This collection of links to primary documents and other resources was compiled by Richard Jensen, a professor emeritus of history at the University of Illinois-Chicago.

Reconstruction Era, http://americanhistory.about.com, part of About.com
This website provides numerous links to resources about Reconstruction.

Index